THE
RULING
CLASS

INSIDE THE
IMPERIAL CONGRESS

ERIC FELTEN

FROM THE HERITAGE FOUNDATION'S
U.S. CONGRESS ASSESSMENT PROJECT
DAVID M. MASON, DIRECTOR

Printed in the United States of America

THE HERITAGE FOUNDATION
214 Massachusetts Avenue, NE
Washington, DC 20002

See coupon on last page of book for bulk copy ordering information.

First printing, January 1993

10 9 8 7 6 5 4

CONTENTS

FOREWORD

The new 103rd Congress has an historic opportunity to help restore confidence in American government. However, it can do so only by restoring confidence in the United States Congress.

That confidence has been shaken to its foundations in recent years, not only by a succession of highly publicized scandals, but by the inability of Congress to do its job.

In the eyes of some critics, Congress's law-making responsibilities now rank far below its other perceived priorities: constituent service, bringing pork home to the state, and appearing on television in the company of Hollywood personalities. The result: a preoccupation with politically popular fads and myths, while the important business of Washington — establishing spending limits and budget priorities, for example — goes begging.

The Heritage Foundation has produced this book because we believe a strong and effective Congress is necessary to the proper functioning of our constitutional democracy. The separation of powers is also critical to that system. The Constitution invests Congress with important powers that it gives no one else. For this reason, Congress has been the principal focus of The Heritage Foundation's research since our founding, in 1973.

As recently as the early seventies, conservatives and liberals alike considered Congress an engine of innovation and change. We conservatives, especially, frequently didn't like the direction in which Congress attempted to lead us, but it usually didn't shy from its duties. Today, however, there seems no more staunch defender of the status quo than Congress. Even legislation that has the apparent support of a majority in both Houses of Congress — such as urban "enterprise zones" — is allowed to stagnate for years because Congress doesn't have the courage to cross swords with entrenched interest groups. The nation is the poorer for this — as is Congress itself.

The Heritage Foundation started examining Congress some five years ago, long before it was politically in vogue. *The Imperial Congress,* which we published jointly with California's Claremont Institute in 1988, provided an historical look at the role of Congress and how the House and Senate had strayed from their constitutional mandate. Subtitled "Crisis in the Separation of Powers," the book argued that Congress had created the current government gridlock: presenting the executive branch with broad mandates, and then second-guessing the executive on the implementation of those mandates. This effort to micromanage the executive was evident throughout the government, from the regulatory agencies to the Pentagon and State Department. *The Imperial Congress* used the analogy of 535 Secretaries of State, each — through the committee hearing process, press releases, subpoena power, and even direct contact with foreign officials (and dissidents) — attempting to establish U.S. foreign policy. Today, we not only have 535 Secretaries of State on Capitol Hill, we also have 535 Secretaries of Defense, Health, Housing, Interior, Labor, Transportation, and just about everything else, and we have thousands of would-be chiefs-of-staff among congressional aides.

The most obvious and needful remedy — and the one we recommended in 1988 — was a vigorous reassertion by the President of his own rights and responsibilities against the encroachment of Congress. We subsequently established the U.S. Congress Assessment Project, to continue and expand this much-needed look at Congress the institution. We have examined the congressional budget process, Congress's own spending and staffing practices, its ethical standards, how campaigns are financed, and the procedures for considering legislation. One conclusion the authors of these studies have unanimously reached: Vigorous executive action in opposing congressional excesses, while essential, is not enough. Congress itself will have to change — its rules and procedures, as well as its incentives and assumptions.

It is not our intention merely to push the pendulum of government power back toward the executive branch.

Conservatives always have been wary of too much power in the hands of a single individual or institution; that's the genius of our system of government. The competition for power between the legislature and executive was designed to limit the government's reach, not to expand it. In fact, re-establishment of a clear separation of powers may serve more to limit the executive than the legislature.

And here lies the point of *The Ruling Class:* It is not the executive branch, or even the government at large, that suffers most from Congress's departure from its constitutional role — it is the Congress itself that's most harmed. This book explores institutional solutions to Congress's institutional problems. Far from engaging in Congress bashing, our intent is to help Congress.

Whether Congress has the will to change things, only history can tell us. If it has that will, *The Ruling Class* will show the way.

EDWIN J. FEULNER, JR., PH.D.
President
THE HERITAGE FOUNDATION

INTRODUCTION

The Ruling Class solves the riddle of why voters hate Congress, but love (or at least reelect) their Congressman — why term limits passed overwhelmingly in the 14 states where it was voted on, yet 93% of the Congressional incumbents on last November's ballot were reelected.

It examines in detail what Congress does, what it doesn't do, and how it operates. It reveals that the United States Congress is a legislature that has stopped legislating, and that this is why Congress doesn't work, and why individual Congressmen escape blame!

Legislation requires votes, which produce accountability. If the results are bad, or not what the public desires, voters can throw the bums out. But today Congress exercises most of its power through methods other than legislation and spends most of its time on nonlegislative pursuits.

The legislation that remains, and the legislative process, is twisted into a convoluted and intentionally confusing mess. *The Ruling Class* sketches out these problems in illuminating detail through telling anecdotes joined to structural analysis.

New faces and even term limits will not alone solve the problems in Congress. Clearly, the entrenched powers will fight to remain in control. Just days after the 1992 Congressional elections House Speaker Tom Foley and other Democratic leaders flew around the country meeting with newly-elected House Democrats.

This unprecedented effort acknowledges the progress that reformers have made, while also serving as a reminder of the challenges still remaining. *The Ruling Class* zeroes in on the structural and institutional changes necessary to rejuvenate the legislative powers of Congress and to restore the political accountability that goes with it. In so doing, the book is a hopeful one. Its advice, if heeded, would restore to Congress the degree of dignity and public approval that our Nation's Founders intended.

If our representatives need encouragement about heeding this advice, this book will contribute to an American public more aware of how Congress operates and, consequently, less easily misled by those who would continue to manipulate Congress and the public.

DAVID M. MASON, DIRECTOR
U.S. Congress Assessment Project
THE HERITAGE FOUNDATION

THE RULING CLASS

In the early hours of Wednesday, November 27, 1991, a string of lawmakers took to the floor of the House of Representatives to declare their support for the Intermodal Surface Transportation Efficiency Act of 1991. Rep. Rosa DeLauro was among them. In the *Congressional Record* is a long speech by the Connecticut Democrat extolling the virtues of what was commonly known as the Highway Bill.

But Rep. DeLauro never did deliver that speech. As a routine matter it was given to the typesetters at the *Congressional Record,* where the text was inserted as though she had spoken at length. So far so good. But somehow the pages of her speech on the Highway Bill became mixed up with the pages of her speech on the Crime Bill. The result was that DeLauro's text jumps from a discussion of all the new jobs that would be created by building roads to comments on a tough gun-control law. She concludes her defense of the Highway Bill by imploring her colleagues to "vote for the Omnibus Crime Control Act."

DeLauro's mixed-up speech is a perfect example of today's Congress: a non-speech that was (not) delivered as part of a non-debate about a bill that no Member had actually read. Indeed, the non-debate on the Highway Bill raced on well before staff aides had even finished writing the bill. Members voted overwhelmingly for the measure without ever seeing it. A hefty thousand pages of small print, the bill was dumped onto a table in the House chamber just one hour before the final vote. This is how Congress spends $151 billion.

$151 billion is a *great* deal of money — more than $1300 in taxes from each and every one of the 112 million taxpayers in America.

Rep. Christopher Cox looked on, astonished. The California Republican sits on the Public Works and Transportation Committee, which drafted the initial House version of the Highway Bill. As a committee member he had hoped to have an intimate knowledge of the bill's details. But not even committee members had the opportunity to read the bill's text. In fact, several months earlier the committee chairman had made the committee vote on the original measure on the same day the several-hundred-page document was passed out. After the committee approved the unread bill, it was sent for the first time to the House floor where only a half dozen amendments were allowed. By the time the measure reached the House-Senate conference committee, the final stage before a bill gets its last up-down vote in each house and is sent to the President, no one but the conference participants knew what the bill would look like. In a conference, leaders from the House and Senate committees that initiated a bill work out the differences between their bodies' respective versions. Because the Senate version of the Highway Bill was wildly different from that approved by the House, everything was up for grabs in the meetings.

And grab they did. Each Member knew there would be some road, bridge, tunnel, sidewalk, bus, or subway earmarked for his home district. Conferees bought their colleagues off with the promise that each legislator would get his own little slice of pork, something to tout when the next election rolled around.

On the afternoon of November 26, the next to last day before Thanksgiving (when Congress planned to close up shop for the year), the leaders of the conference announced they had reached an agreement. They then handed out a two-page outline of the thousand-page bill. Staff aides were still busy writing up the compromise text. Although Cox tried to get the conference staff to show him the measure, they told him he would have to wait. Around 2:00 a.m. on the 27th, the bill was taken up by the House Rules Committee, which sets the ground rules for debate on legislation before it is sent to the floor, specifying what amendments can be considered and in what order.

In the case of the Highway Bill, however, there was not much point in specifying amendments because the Rules Committee itself did not have a copy of the measure, which was still being drawn up. Without having seen the bill, the Rules Committee waived the House requirement that no measure be taken up until three days after it has been printed in the *Congressional Record*. They then sent the bill to the floor.

At 4:00 a.m. debate began — though no one had yet seen the text. Not until nearly 5:00 a.m., halfway through the debate, was one copy of the document plunked down on the Speaker's table. There it sat, more than one-thousand pages, until 6:00 a.m., when the vote was taken. Approval was overwhelming, 372 Members voted for the bill and only 47 opposed. Not a single Member, Cox realized, had read it.

This is all too typical of how today's Congress legislates, with empty votes on bills known only to unelected staff aides, all crammed into the last hours before vacation. Legislation has become the stepchild of Capitol Hill. Cumbersome and difficult, legislating requires coalitions and compromises. How much easier it is for lawmakers to act without having to legislate. Just call a bureaucrat and demand a favor for a constituent; write a regulator and insist that a federal rule be changed; hold a hearing and drum up some press; fly to the Third World and exercise a little personal diplomacy. Congress was created to make laws; yet the modern Congress has all but abandoned legislating, choosing instead to exercise power more directly and with less accountability.

Welcome to the Ruling Class, whose members have become the barons in an Imperial Congress where the protection and expansion of personal fiefdoms outweigh the needs of the nation. Deceit, calumny, and character assassination are commonplace as our representatives strive to augment their power. Washington has been poisoned with their machinations and our political system sickened as well.

1
SLEIGHT OF HAND

It has been said here many times tonight that we want to make the Senate the same as everyone else, that we want to treat Senators the same as everyone else, that we want to have the Senate treated the same as the private sector.

Mr. President, not a single Senator believes that. Not a single Senator wants that.

Senate Democratic Leader George
Mitchell explaining why the Senate
should not be covered by a major civil
rights bill.

House Democrats would love to send Rep. Newt Gingrich back to his life as a journeyman college professor. The feisty Georgia Republican represents one of the few real threats to the Democrats' domination of the House of Representatives. Yet in the fall of 1990, when the Democrats had their chance to get rid of Gingrich, they gave him a pass. Gingrich had voted for a congressional pay raise, a fact that his opponent, Democrat David Worley made the centerpiece of his campaign. Polls showed Worley nearing a major upset. But then his own party's congressional campaign committee cut off his supply of campaign cash, and Worley lost. Why did the Democrats starve out Worley and give up the chance to knock off their nemesis? Because they had promised to: The same pay raise that nearly cost Gingrich his seat ended up saving it for him.

So universal is the need to cover up a pay grab, that it is one of the few issues that can bind Congress together in a display of bipartisan unity. When a cleverly crafted salary boost for Representatives teetered on the verge of collapse in 1990, Democratic and Republican leaders signed a "non-aggression pact": neither party's congressional campaign committee would give any money to challengers who made the pay raise a campaign issue. When Worley questioned the pay raise, his party disowned him. If collusion on this scale were practiced by makers of paper clips, rather than makers of law, they would be in jail.

The public hates it when lawmakers hike their own pay. But legislators, usually slavish followers of opinion polls, are not about to be chastened by public opinion when it comes to an issue so dear to their hearts. But how do Members of Congress get away with voting for things the public despises? They use camouflage.

For the most part, lawmakers need not resort to such means as the non-aggression pact. Usually, technical language and obscure legalisms will do the trick. How else does one explain this provision in the 1992 legislative appropriations bill:

The rate of pay for the offices referred to under section 703 (a) (2) (B) of the Ethics Reform Act of 1989 (5 U.S.C. 5318 note) shall be the rate of pay that would be payable for each such office if the provisions of section 703 (a) (2) (B) and 1101 (a) (1) (A) of such act (5 U.S.C. 5318 note and 5305) had not been enacted.

Translation: Senators get a $23,200-a-year raise.

Unfortunately for taxpayers, arcane wording is not the only trick up Congress's sleeve. Through a variety of procedural sleights of hand, Members of Congress mislead their constituents and evade accountability. Votes, alas, require lawmakers to take stands. And so Congressmen have found innumerable ways to get around votes. Perhaps the most insidious and most frequently used trick is to let conference committees — the groups assigned to work out differences between House and Senate versions of a bill — do the dirty work.

The 1990 Chapman Amendment to the Americans with Disabilities Act (ADA) is a case in point. The amendment would have allowed restaurants to move cooks and waiters with AIDS into jobs where they wouldn't handle food. Although both Houses of Congress supported the amendment, it somehow never made it into the final bill. This incensed Rep. William Dannemeyer. "The Chapman Amendment was adopted on the floor of the House after a big debate," the California Republican told the House. "The Senate...instructed its conferees to adopt the same language, and...when the conferees got together on this measure, they totally ignored it."

Rep. Hamilton Fish, one of the conferees accused of ignoring the will of the House and Senate, leaped to his feet to defend himself. "The simple fact is that there were some 81 or 82 issues between the Senate and the House; 79 of these were resolved by the staffs prior to the Members meeting in conference, so there were only two or three issues to be considered, and one of them was the Chapman Amendment, and it was the burden of the time spent," said the New York Republican.

Fish was right; the conferees had not ignored the Chapman Amendment. What they did was draw a careful bead on the measure and pull the trigger. Conference committees are supposed to address the differences between the two houses over a piece of legislation in order to work out a compromise. But in this case, and in many like it, conferees ignore how Congress voted and rewrite the bill as they want.

But why, if the will of the Congress had been trampled by the conferees, did both houses vote to adopt the conferees' version of the bill? Perhaps for the same reason both houses voted to adopt a conference report in 1989 that included millions of dollars for congressional mass mailings, though both houses had gone on record opposing such mailings. And maybe for the same reason the Senate and House approved a conference bill in 1991 that allowed National Endowment for the Arts funding for excrementitious artworks, again against the stated preference of both the House and Senate.

Could it be that conferees are simply doing what Congress wants them to do? That our representatives are teases, saying no when they mean yes and yes when they mean no?

The short answer is yes. Harvard government professor Morris Fiorina explains this phenomenon in his *Congress,*

Keystone of the Washington Establishment. Over the last 30 years, legislators have discovered that, by concentrating on constituent service (everything from intervening for a voter in his dispute with the IRS to helping out a constituent's child in a homework assignment), they can build enough good will to put themselves out of electoral striking distance of any challenger. As we will see in examining the sources of incumbents' electoral strength, add the hallowed pork barrel to constituent service and you get a reelection rate near 100 percent.

Voting is one of the few activities that ever threatens to wrench this nifty reelection machine: Whereas constituent service makes almost everyone happy, a vote on even a mildly divisive issue is sure to annoy a number of voters.

Nowhere is congressional vote-avoidance more obvious than when Congress and the voters both feel strongly about an issue and yet come down on different sides. Take the question of lawmakers' mass mailings. Most Members of Congress are devoted to the frank, which allows them to mass-mail "newsletters" as well as respond to constituent inquiries, all without the inconvenience of paying for stamps. Voters rightly think of this as another boondoggle that should be abolished. On the surface, it looks as though there's no real way out: It's one or the other. Except in Congress, that is. Lawmakers rigged the voting mechanism so that Members could pretend to do the popular thing while reversing themselves when no one was looking. They voted against the frank and took the mail out the back door.

This little dance began in early September 1989, when Sen. Pete Wilson, a California Republican, saw an opportunity to rid voters' mailboxes of congressional junk mail (and at the same time do a little pre-season grandstanding in his bid for the California governor's chair). Senators were wrapping up their debate on the 1990 legislative appropriations bill (which funds their mail and other congressional expenses) when Wilson offered an amendment cutting Congress's postage budget from $134.7 million to $35 million, of which only $4 million could be used in 1990.

Wilson's measure might have scored fewer votes had he not wired it to the hot-button issue of the year: drugs. Democrats had been making fun of the Republican drug strategy, caricaturing it as a combination of fruitless self-improvement hype ("Just Say No") and dangerous police-state tactics. Treatment for addicts, they were saying, was the way to win the war on drugs. So Wilson offered an amendment that not only cut funding for franking, but spent the savings on drug treatment *for pregnant women.* Senators had to choose, publicly, between personal privilege and crack babies. Of course, babies won, 83-8.

House Members got a chance to choose as well, with a September 25 motion telling House conferees to agree to the Wilson Amendment. This is known as a "motion to instruct," which is non-binding. Because conferees can choose to ignore them, such motions represent one of the best sources of free votes: Lawmakers can go on record supporting Policy X knowing that, with a wink and a nod, the conferees will ignore their instructions. So without too much concern the House voted by a solid 245-137 margin to acquiesce to the Senate position slashing franking funds. A scant three hours later, conferees cut a deal to restore the mass mailings.

Three days after the House had voted to end mass mailings, the body overwhelmingly approved a conference-reported bill which included $84 million for just such mail. In a 274-137 vote, over 100 Representatives who had opposed the mailings supported the bill as a whole.

This kind of trickery helps Congress maintain one of its most blatant double standards: Members are exempt from most of the laws, rules, and regulations they inflict on the rest of us. The Americans with Disabilities Act (ADA), for instance, might have applied to Congress had it not been for another creative use of conference committees, which allowed Congress to claim it was covered while escaping effective enforcement.

In his acceptance speech at the 1988 Republican National Convention George Bush had promised to "do whatever it takes to make sure the disabled are included in the mainstream." Unlike his campaign pledge of "No new taxes," when the ADA was reported to the Senate floor at the end of August 1989, Bush honored his promise to support it. With the backing of both the White House and Democrats on the Hill, the ADA would have raced through the Senate save for an inconvenient amendment by Sen. Charles Grassley. The Iowa Republican had long been pursuing a concern that traces itself back to James Madison in Federalist No. 57. There, Madison had warned that Congress could be kept from passing oppressive measures only if "they can make no law which will not have its full operation on themselves and their friends, as well as on the great mass of the society." Madison stressed that by living under the same laws as the governed, legislators would have a "communion of interests and sympathy of sentiments... without which every government degenerates into tyranny." Grassley pointed out that Congress had exempted itself from the most important pieces of modern legislation: the Civil Rights Act of 1964, the Freedom of Information Act of 1966, the Age Discrimination Act of 1967, the Occupational Safety and Health Act of 1970, the Equal Employment Opportunity Act of 1972, Title 9 of the Higher Education Act of 1972, the Rehabilitation Act of 1973, the Privacy Act of 1974, the Age Discrimination Act Amendments of 1975, the Ethics in Government Act of 1978, and the Civil Rights Restoration Act of 1988.

The amendment Grassley offered went straight to the point. It said simply that the ADA would apply to the Senate. Offered late in the evening, there were few present on the Senate floor to object. Sen. Wendell Ford emitted the stock congressional response: allowing the executive branch to bring charges against a Member of Congress for employment discrimination would be an unconstitutional violation of the separation of powers.

Notwithstanding Ford's complaints, Grassley's amendment passed on a voice vote of the few Senators actually on the floor at that hour. Grassley's success was due in large part to the support of Sen. Tom Harkin, Chairman of the Disability Policy Subcommittee and prime sponsor of the ADA. The Iowa Democrat was for the amendment for somewhat different reasons than Grassley. By making Congress subject to the same burdens, Grassley hoped to make lawmakers think carefully about the burdens they were imposing on the private sector. Harkin, on the other hand, whose brother is deaf, was committed to imposing the toughest rules everywhere, even on Capitol Hill.

Yet Harkin still gave his colleagues a wink. Even though they were voting to cover Congress just like any business, they needn't worry. In conference he would work it out so that "it is Congress, the legislative branch, that enforces the provisions of the act."

The conference delivered on part of Harkin's promise. The court of first resort for those with complaints against a Senator was to be the Senate's own disciplinary review board. But the kicker was that those not satisfied with the Senate's justice could appeal to federal court. Panicked cries resounded throughout the Senate. Two weeks later, the conference report was sent back to conferees, this time with explicit instructions not to allow appeals beyond the Senate.

Parliament of Tricksters

Most real House business is conducted in the Committee of the Whole, where, until 1970, most formal votes on amendments were so-called teller votes: House Members formed two lines, one for yes and one for no. The number of Representatives for and against a measure was recorded, but how individual Members voted was not.

Liberals blamed the teller voting system for a string of losses on crucial votes that they believed would have gone their way had the votes been subject to public scrutiny. Tip O'Neill, the Massachusetts Democrat who later became Speaker of the House, proposed an amendment to the Legislative Reorganization Act of 1970 to allow individual Member's votes to be recorded on teller votes. "The secrecy of the Committee of the Whole has allowed too many Members to duck issues, to avoid the perils of controversial votes," he said. "But that is not in the spirit of this Nation, nor of this Congress." He went on to cite votes that he was sure would have gone the other way if legislators had to vote on the record. "The ABM, the SST, the invasion of Cambodia, were all dealt with in the Committee of the Whole, in non-recorded teller votes."

O'Neill did not expect recorded votes to be demanded often, and, of course, he and the liberals who pushed the measure through expected to win most of them. It didn't turn out that way. During the 1971-72 sessions of Congress in which O'Neill's rule was first put in force, there were 193 recorded votes in the Committee of the Whole. Six years later the 95th Congress saw 505 such votes. And the explosion of recorded votes was not working to the liberals' advantage.

With Republicans using high-profile votes on divisive issues to embarrass Democrats during election season, the same Democrats who had fought to bring the process under the klieg lights of public debate now turned to the Rules Committee to save them from the democratic monster they had created. In the late 1950s the House Rules Committee had been controlled by a coalition of Republicans and conservative Southern Democrats who frustrated civil rights efforts by keeping much of the movement's legislation from coming to the floor. In 1961 that hold was loosened when a majority of Members joined Speaker Sam Rayburn to expand the size of the committee, putting a number of new, and more liberal, Members on it. Still unhappy with the way the old guard on the Rules Committee was using so-called closed rules to keep liberal initiatives from being voted on, Democrats changed their rules in 1973 to make instructions from the Democratic Caucus binding on Democratic members of the committee.

Now that they were in control of the committee, Democrats found that a variety of closed and semi-closed rules could be used to frustrate the Republicans' agenda, and they quickly proved they had no qualms about doing so. In the 95th Congress (1977-78) only 15 percent of the rules restricted what amendments could be offered; by 1991, the first year of the 102nd Congress, 61 percent of rules limited amendments and debate. Democrats insist that the restrictive rules are used to bring order to an institution made chaotic by democratic reforms. But Republicans complain that the rules are almost exclusively partisan.

The ultimate in stealth legislation is House Rule XLIX. Congress's inability to control spending has been an embarrassment to lawmakers, particularly Democrats. Nowhere has that embarrassment been more keenly felt than in the need to raise the federal debt ceiling. Each year, sometimes more than once a year, Congress has to vote to hike the debt limit as the federal deficit grows. Republicans have made much of the votes, refusing to increase debt and castigating those Democrats who did. Many Democrats, desperate to look fiscally responsible, defected on the votes, endangering the majority's ability to keep the financing flowing. The Democrats needed a solution. But instead of cutting spending, they came up with the perfect out, Rule XLIX.

Now a standing rule of the House, XLIX raises the debt ceiling automatically. When Congress adopts its annual budget resolution, which almost always increases the deficit more than is allowed by the statutory limit on borrowing, the House no longer has to go on record as voting for the debt limit to go up. Instead, "the vote by which the conference report on the concurrent resolution on the budget was agreed to in the House… shall be deemed to have been a vote in favor" of raising the debt ceiling. In other words, Congress now has turned to voting without voting. How can a Representative be held accountable for votes he's only *deemed* to have made?

No more than he can be held accountable for votes that never come to pass, here's another nifty trick that can be arranged in the House. Often Members sign up as cosponsors of bills which they do not really favor. They can point out the cosponsorship to voters all the while knowing that the relevant committee chairman will bottle up the measure so that it will never get voted upon. When this happens, Members may sign what is known as a discharge petition. If a majority of lawmakers sign the petition, the bill is kicked out of the committee and comes up for a vote. So an easy way to tell if a legislator favors a stalled bill to see if he has signed the discharge petition. Unfortunately, the names on the petition are kept strictly confidential. The signatures are so secret that Members who leak them are to be punished.

Can there be any reason for this secrecy other than to protect lawmakers from the scrutiny of their constituents? Since the late '80s, more than half the Members of the House listed themselves as supporters of a bill to amend the Constitution to require a balanced federal budget. Yet there were never enough signatures on the discharge petition to bring the measure up for a vote until the spring of 1992. Clearly someone was lying.

2

THE BULLIES' PULPIT

We merely take testimony.

Rep. Tom Lantos explaining that it did
not matter that Members of Congress
were duped on national TV.

Remember the Great Alar Scare of 1989?

That February, CBS's *60 Minutes* charged that
Alar — a growth-regulating chemical used widely on
apples — was causing an epidemic of cancer deaths,
with children being at particular risk. "The most potent
cancer-causing agent in our food supply," intoned
correspondent Ed Bradley, "is a substance sprayed
on apples to keep them on the trees longer and make
them look better." In the panic that ensued, apples, apple
juice, applesauce, and apple pies were pulled from store
shelves and school lunch-counters.

There was nothing to the scare, of course. Alar is perfectly safe. But the scare was not without its price: Apple growers estimate they lost somewhere between $60 million and $140 million.

Nor was the scare innocent. The Alar panic occurred because of a publicity stunt staged by Congress and a special-interest group. The *60 Minutes* broadcast had been arranged by David Fenton, whose firm, Fenton Communications, was being paid more than $180,000 a year to promote the anti-Alar campaign of the Natural Resources Defense Council (NRDC). The network had been given exclusive use of a new NRDC report on Alar and other agricultural chemicals. The report was called "Intolerable Risk: Pesticides in Our Children's Food," and CBS played it to the hilt.

Now, one scary story on TV is a good start, but anti-Alar hysteria would never have taken off without team-work: the combined efforts of federal regulatory agencies, interest groups, and Congress are needed to yield such bountiful press coverage. In the case of Alar, Fenton had also arranged that one week after *60 Minutes* gave credence to the NRDC charges, actress Meryl Streep would announce the formation of a citizens' group called "Mothers and Others for Pesticide Limits."

Within a month of the *60 Minutes* story the Senate Subcommittee on Children, Family, Drugs and Alcoholism, chaired by Connecticut Democrat Christopher Dodd, had arranged a hearing. The hearing had every publicity ingredient: child victims, a press in full gallop, and, best of all, an honest-to-goodness movie star, Meryl Streep. It didn't even matter that they couldn't produce any actual children who had become sick because of

Alar. It was enough to talk solemnly about the thousands "at risk."

The hearing provided for such juicy publicity that it attracted Senators who were not members of Dodd's subcommittee. Connecticut Democrat Sen. Joseph Lieberman, for example, put in a guest appearance to ask Streep a few fawning questions. Even Sen. Brock Adams, a Democrat from the apple-growing state of Washington, went along with the hype, arguing that the problem was with the chemical's manufacturer rather than with the apple farmers: "Uniroyal ... would do us all a great public service if they suspended production of the chemical until controversy on the product safety is resolved," said Adams. "That allows the processors and those who are using apple products to avoid boycotts."

The lone sour note came from Sen. Steve Symms, a third-generation apple-grower. The Idaho Republican suggested that the environmentalists' report was absurd, And he was right. The NRDC's risk estimates had been produced by exaggerating the results of a study that had itself been discredited. The previous report, the Toth study, had been rejected in 1985 by an EPA Scientific Advisory Panel: the mice in the study had been fed such extraordinary high levels of Alar that they were dying from the sheer toxicity of the dose. The NRDC combined the Toth figures with high estimates of the amount of apples consumed by children, and came up with the alarming conclusion that as many as 910 children per million would get cancer from Alar. By comparison, a study by the California Department of Food and Agriculture found that Alar use had a probable lifetime cancer risk of only 3.5 per trillion.

With most such hypes, a few lawmakers will break ranks and do some debunking. But the Alar case is instructive, because such skepticism usually owes itself (as with Symms) to a personal or constituent reason rather than any general commitment to sound science. In cases in which a constituent's ox is gored — such as apple growers in Washington state — a lawmaker does not have to struggle to burst the hype. Like Brock Adams, all he has to do is redirect the fire toward someone else's constituents; in this case, pointing the finger not at the apple growers who used Alar but the chemical manufacturers who produced it. Or, in best huckster fashion, a lawmaker can play along, reap the publicity benefits, and overcome constituent concerns with... more publicity.

Look at how Sen. Tom Harkin handled an exchange with Meryl Streep. "There are those who think that this hysteria — you have addressed that, this is not hysteria, that it is based upon facts," the Iowa Democrat said, after commending the actress for being present. Clearly the farm-state Senator was not about to assail the contention that agricultural chemicals pose huge dangers to children. But how could he pacify his farmer constituents, who rely on such chemicals for their livelihood?

> **Sen. Harkin:** Let me just ask you a very personal question. I have been contacted by the Iowa Farm Bureau. They are in town today. Would you be willing to meet with some farm families and talk to them?
>
> **Ms. Streep:** Yes, I would love to, as a matter of fact, yes.

Sen. Harkin: Would you come out and meet with some farm families?

Ms. Streep: Yes, absolutely.

Streep never actually went to Iowa to meet with farm families, but just getting her to say she would was good enough for some TV clips.

The Alar hearing did not result in legislation. But it didn't have to. The flip-side of all the good publicity for the Senators and the NRDC was bad publicity for apple-growers and for Uniroyal. Under pressure, the chemical company withdrew Alar from the market. Thus lawmakers were able to speak out on behalf of victims without having to follow through with actual legislation (which might have required looking at the NRDC's claims more carefully).

Though probably one of the more notorious, Alar is by no means the only innocent scalp taken by Congress and special-interest groups in their collaborative efforts to produce publicity. Again and again the groups and legislators work together to build media hypes and keep themselves in the spotlight. The special-interest groups provide the scripts, and the lawmakers provide the stage. Alar was the Tony Award winner in this Broadway on the Potomac.

Such shows are one of Congress's most versatile weapons. For one thing, they can help Members play catch-up when they've been left behind on a high-profile issue. Hearings in October 1990 on Iraqi military atrocities exemplified this.

As hostilities between the U.S.-led allies and Iraqi strongman Saddam Hussein continued to escalate,

Democrats had been dragging their feet. But when it became clear that the White House was going to take military action, and — more importantly — that the public supported such a move, the lawmakers rushed to jump on the bandwagon. The Congressional Human Rights Caucus used its hearings to cover the change of heart.

The centerpiece of the hearings, chaired by California Democrat Tom Lantos, was testimony by "Nayirah." Nayirah was a 15-year-old Kuwaiti girl who broke into tears as she told of seeing Iraqi soldiers steal maternity-ward incubators, leaving infants to die on the hospital floor. This tale of shocking cruelty became a refrain in the speeches of lawmakers justifying their support for action in the Persian Gulf. But though Iraqis committed thousands of brutal crimes against Kuwaitis, stealing incubators does not seem to have been among them.

Nayirah's real name was kept a secret, ostensibly to protect her family. As it turned out, her family was already a high-profile target: Nayirah's father was the Kuwaiti ambassador to the United States, Saud Nasir al-Sabah. Rep. Lantos kept that fact under wraps, along with information that her appearance had been arranged by Kuwait's public-relations firm, Hill and Knowlton. Had Nayirah's real identity been known, it might have led some lawmakers to be more skeptical (for the same reasons one ought to be skeptical of industry research, or any other self-interested information).

Not until after the war were reporters able to investigate Nayirah's claims by asking Kuwaiti doctors about the theft of incubators. No evidence could be found to confirm the girl's account. When it finally got out that Nayirah was the ambassador's daughter, Lantos was asked why he had so unskeptically accepted her story. "Whether every single claimed human rights violation took place exactly the way the claim was made is utterly secondary," he responded. "We merely take testimony." Even under false pretenses, it appears.

Hearings have still other functions. For one, they can be used to embarrass administration officials with whom lawmakers disagree — a sort of bullies' pulpit. Congress has expanded its power over the last 20 years, not through far-reaching legislation, but through informal means, such as phone calls to federal regulators demanding that agency rules be written this way or that. The bullies' pulpit is crucial to this back-channel way of doing business. Much of Congress's informal power comes from its ability to punish foes by making them look foolish (or worse) on national television.

Witnesses subpoenaed by congressional committees frequently are not allowed to have lawyers present when they testify. And when they do have attorneys, private conversations with them are often prohibited: Congress, unlike the courts or the executive, does not respect the lawyer-client privilege of confidentiality.

Electronic Boilerplate

In our media age, one of the greatest advantages an incumbent has is the ability to get himself on television. As Congress has increasingly tooled up as a reelection machine, lawmakers have become ever more sophisticated media hounds. Twenty years ago, only one in eight Member of the House had full-time press secretaries. Today, well over half do. Nor are these press secretaries' jobs as limited as they once were. They do not simply send out press releases and set up interviews for reporters. Sometimes they pretend to be journalists themselves.

Each Wednesday afternoon a crowd of legislators can be found on the lawn in front of the east side of the Capitol. Camera crews from both parties' congressional campaign committees roll video tape while Members are interviewed... by their own press secretaries. The interviews are edited down to usable sound bites and beamed back to home district TV stations, where, more often than not, the electronic boilerplate is presented as if it were the products of a news team.

These Wednesday afternoon interviews are but one example of one of the least known, but most useful, perks of congressional office: subsidized media production. Not only do taxpayers foot the bill for franked mail that serves as little more than advertisements for incumbents, they pay for House and Senate television studios. Although most electronic boilerplate for home district radio and television stations is produced at the studios run by the campaign committees (paid for with private donations), the Senate Recording and Photographic Studios still have over 60 employees with combined salaries of over $2 million. The House TV operation includes 20 production people, 10 cameramen, two TV studios, and four radio studios.

The reason these operations are so important is that the all-important "media hit" is critical for reelection. Lawmakers don't look for hits on the national media;

network congressional coverage is usually limited to the party leaders and those lawmakers who are in the news because they are running for President.

In their own districts, however, Members of Congress are celebrities. Incumbents have several times the visibility of challengers, thanks largely to their more frequent appearances in the press and on radio and TV. The annual National Election Study asks constituents whether they had seen or heard of their congressional candidates in any of a variety of ways. Half of the respondents had read about the incumbent in the newspaper; only one in five had seen mention of the challenger. A fourth of the voters had heard the incumbent on the radio; less than one in 10 had heard the challenger. More than one half had seen the incumbent on television; less than a fifth had seen the challenger.

This incumbent visibility is created, in no small part, through the barrage of video and audio "feeds," as the electronic boilerplate is known. Local stations eagerly snap up the material. They do so partly because their budgets are too limited to afford their own coverage of Washington. They also like the information supplied from Congress because, unlike network coverage, it is customized for their audiences. The feeds may not be objective, but for local stations trying to fill air time, they are better than nothing. So vital to reelection have these video feeds become that Hedrick Smith calls them the first of his "Five Pillars of Incumbency."

Not that Members of Congress ignore newspapers. Many congressional offices put out what are called "slicks," press releases produced to look exactly like an op-ed column in a newspaper. Slicks come complete with photos and headlines all ready to be pasted into a newspaper. Most larger metropolitan newspapers look down on this prepackaged copy, but many smaller dailies or local weeklies are happy to have their congressional coverage provided to them free.

Hearings add a "news" angle to such coverage. "The value of a hearing as a propaganda channel is that it is an event," wrote congressional scholar David Truman in 1971. "It is news. Especially when the participants are prominent or the testimony involves startling revelations or sharp conflicts, the event is likely to receive generous coverage in the media. At some points in the development of a measure, in fact, the primary purpose of hearings lies in their propaganda value."

If hearings implied an opening of the government to the citizens, the attendant evils of congressional grandstanding would be easier to abide. As with pay raises, and tricky rules, however, lawmakers go to great lengths to muddy the media waters when it comes to substantive and controversial issues. Real legislation tends to have losers as well as winners, and taking a public stand means angering the losers. Better to seek publicity on issues without much of a downside. This is where victims come in handy.

Victims make compelling news; just look at *Geraldo*, *Oprah*, or *Donahue*. Members of Congress know this better than anyone, and they do their best to oblige by cramming their hearings full of victims. Their stories are frequently engrossing, but only rarely do they have any relevance to serious public policy. In fact, the very hunt for victims and the publicity they provide almost guarantee that consideration of real policy issues is excluded.

Thus do members of Congress buy into an endless succession of environmental, consumer, and public-health scams.

It's not always easy to find victims, even with the vast staffs Members have, and here is where the public-interest lobbies play their part. These groups represent a variety of interests, from environmental groups and Ralph Nader-affiliated consumer organizations to civil-rights and public-health organizations. These groups also depend on publicity, and appearing at congressional hearings represents a rich source of exposure. These ad hoc relationships are at the heart of a new power structure on Capitol Hill, a structure so dependent on cheap showmanship that we might call it the Barnumocracy.

Victims were out in force at a March 26, 1990, House hearing on the diet industry. Rep. Ron Wyden, an Oregon Democrat, was ring-master. His Small Business Subcommittee on Regulation, Business Opportunities, and Energy had convened the hearings to discuss whether the diet industry was putting the nation at risk. The answer must have been yes, given the complaints of the opening panel. Loretta Pameijer testified that her daughter's gallbladder had to be removed a few months after she had gone on the Doctor's Quick Weight Loss Center program. Sherri Steinberg blamed her attack of gallstones on Nutri/System. That company was also blamed for the heart attack and consequent brain damage of Carol Householder's husband.

Certainly these are tragic stories, and it's impossible not to sympathize with the women. But that sympathy all too easily displaces the questions of how and why the injuries really happened. For example, it was not clear whether Mr. Householder suffered his heart attack because of his diet or because he was exercising too strenuously. Similarly, were the gallbladder difficulties suffered by the two women the result of a loss in weight or the fact that these women had previously been overweight? (There is a higher incidence of gallstones among the obese as well as among those losing weight.) The women could not answer those questions. In fact, they could offer no medical evidence that the diets had been at fault.

That didn't matter. It didn't matter, because answers never do in hearings. The network news picked up the story, complete with the suggestion that the health of all dieters was seriously at risk. The hearing got so much publicity that Nutri/System had to take out advertisements in major national newspapers detailing the safety of their diet program. The company had not been invited to the hearing; according to a spokesman for Rep. Wyden, the event was put together on such short notice that Nutri/System would not have had time to prepare its testimony. It would have been unfair to the company to have them appear.

No legislation was passed as a result of the hearing, but in Wyden's office the diet event is considered a paradigm of congressional success. It is also a paradigm of the Barnumocracy. Rep. Wyden's staff did not go out searching for people who had been stricken by faulty diets. Instead, his staff was approached by lawyers representing plaintiffs in lawsuits against the diet industry. The lawyers provided the script and the cast and helped whip up publicity for the congressional show. In return, public pressure to settle built up on the objects of their lawsuits.

The media are crucial to the success of these efforts. And, although the press has a reputation for cynicism and street smarts, reporters are not all that hard to manipulate. Take the road show put on jointly by Rep. Charles Schumer, a New York Democrat, and Allstate Insurance. At hearings in his New York district, and then on Capitol Hill, Schumer staged the dismantling of an automobile. Allstate supplied the cars, the mechanics, and the statistics on the value of the cannibalized parts. The New York stunt prompted coverage in the *New York Post,* the *Daily News,* and on all the local television stations. The Washington exhibition succeeded as well with stories in the *Washington Post* and on *ABC Nightly News*.

The *Washington Post* article was typical of the ease with which journalists are taken in by exaggerated claims. "Over the next 10 minutes, off came wheel covers ($1,489.18), the four doors ($13,257.80), the front assembly ($7,288.62), and the seats ($4,895.19), the *Post* reported. "When it was all over, the 1990 Cadillac Brougham d'Elegance was worth far more in pieces than it was whole — $35,740 compared with the book value of $20,800.

The reporter never thought to ask, why, if 10 minutes' effort could turn a $20,800 car into $35,740 worth of parts, there isn't a booming legal business in buying Cadillacs and taking them apart. Or, why is the "street" value of hubcaps one thousand four hundred eighty-nine dollars *and eighteen cents?* Are we to believe there is a hoodlums' parts catalogue in which the items are priced out to the penny? If the press cannot dredge up some skepticism when the publicity factor is this transparent, it is no wonder the Barnumocracy functions so smoothly.

It is not difficult to see why Allstate did its part in the car stunt. After all, insurers hate getting stuck with the bill for replacing stripped or stolen cars. It is less obvious, initially, why the public-interest lobbies play their part in the hyping of health scares and the like. It is argued that the Nader groups, such as Public Citizen, are funded to some extent by trial lawyers, and thus are motivated to aid litigators who profit from the lawsuits the scares promote. That may be the case. The more plausible explanation is twofold. First, the groups enjoy, and need, publicity themselves. Second, their visibility and public relations skills make them invaluable congressional allies, a service for which they are well and variously rewarded by Congress.

Scholars like David Truman recognized that hearings could be used as propaganda but thought the publicity would be used primarily to advance legislation. Little could one have predicted that the "legislative process" would be corrupted to the point where legislation frequently is irrelevant. It's the show that matters. And it's all built on the assumption that we are the suckers P.T. Barnum took us for.

3

LEGISLATING BACKWARDS

> *We create the government that screws you, and then you're supposed to thank us for protecting you from it.*
>
> —Rep. Vin Weber (R-Minn.)

If Congress spends most of its time trying to evade difficult choices and participating in overly dramatic but largely fruitless hearings, then how do the laws get made? Someone else does it, of course, and that someone is usually a bureaucrat.

A major element of congressional sleight of hand is to write hopelessly vague and contradictory laws, which delegate broad legislative authority to the federal bureaucracy. The agencies then have to make the rules and regulations, the legal specifics that step on people's toes. This process of legislating without actually passing laws allows Congress to avoid accountability. But this doesn't mean that lawmakers actually leave the rule-making process to the bureaucrats. Legislators want to have their say, and have given special interests their say as well. To make sure that their friends in the public lobbies get the regulations they desire, Congress has devised a number of ways for lobbyists to intervene in rulemaking, of which the most recent invention is the so-called "regulation negotiation" or "reg neg."

The idea of a reg-neg is that all the parties interested in a given regulation get together and hash out a deal with the respective federal agency. In exchange for having a hand in shaping the rule, the interests promise not to challenge the regulation in court. Professors of administrative law defend this development, claiming that because all interests are represented the regulations can't help but be fair. But they are wrong, for several reasons. To begin with, it is a mistake to think that businesses are always anti-regulation. Many firms thrive on the fact that bureaucratic red tape strangles their rivals. Marriott Hotels, for example, eagerly, and successfully, pushed for tough standards during a regulation negotiation under the Americans with Disabilities Act. The hotel chain had been building its lodgings to be handicapped-friendly for more than 10 years. Making compliance with such architectural standards federal law was a boon to the company: It would not have to change a thing, whereas the firm's competitors would have to spend millions to meet the new rules.

But the biggest problem with the idea that reg-neg is a fair alternative to real legislation is the assumption that democracy can be replaced by special-interest haggling. So comfortable has Congress become in doing the bidding of special interests that is sees no problem with simply handing over to them the task of legislating. The legislative process intended to tame the influence of factions has been abandoned. In the Barnumocracy, factions rule.

This habit of delegating legislative powers is the key to understanding how the federal government has grown so large. The divisions of power in the Constitution were designed not only to guard against tyranny. More fundamentally, the separation of powers made governing difficult. It required that government action be taken through an unwieldy and tortuous legislative process. These procedural constraints narrowed the scope of federal power.

Today these pesky constraints have been discarded. The courts bear some of the blame for the blurring of the Constitutional boundaries. But the bulk of the blame rests on the shoulders of Congress: In its efforts to facilitate President Franklin Roosevelt's New Deal, Capitol Hill handled over sweeping legislative powers to the chief executive and his agencies. The division of powers was purposefully short-circuited.

Congress came to regret this as it saw its power shrink in comparison to what came to be known by the late 1960s as the "Imperial Presidency." But Congress has been unwilling to take its lawmaking powers back, as incumbents realized that the abdication actually helped them get reelected. If bureaucrats make the laws, they are the ones who get blamed for the costs and inconveniences those laws might cause. Lawmakers, in turn, gain credit by fixing problems the bureaucracy has caused for their constituents.

OSHA is a case in point. The 1973 statute that created the Occupational Safety and Health Administration required OSHA to take every existing industry guideline on health and safety, and make it a federal regulation. When the agency did just that, and the rules began to pinch, OSHA took the heat. But rather than blame Congress, business looked to legislators for relief, and called on them to rein in the agency. By expanding federal powers and promoting onerous regulation, Congress had not brought itself under criticism. It had cleverly created for itself new clients for constituent service: businesses who needed relief from OSHA.

This institutionalized buck-passing persists, especially with high-profile laws that amount to little more than the legislation of nice sentiments. Such is the case with the Americans with Disabilities Act (ADA).

Businesses are required to provide "reasonable accommodations" to workers with disabilities as long as that doesn't cause the firm "undue hardship." Sen. Tom Harkin, the Iowa Democrat who led the fight for the ADA, tried to define what undue hardship meant when asked on the Senate floor if the provision would require, for example, that a company provide a full-time reader for a blind employee. "If it is IBM, perhaps that is not a big deal. But if it is a small pharmacy, … that's a different story," he answered. What kind of guide is that? How are medium-sized businesses to know if they are abiding by the law? Though a law is hopelessly vague, at least the agencies can issue regulations. But in the case of the ADA, even the agencies have balked on defining the key terms, explicitly leaving it to the courts to decide.

The final rules for the ADA set out by the Equal Employment Opportunity Commission (EEOC) simply paraphrase the ambiguities in the law. Examples are given to illustrate what might be considered a "reasonable accommodation," but even they are couched in uncertain terms. Consider this illustration given by the EEOC:

> Suppose an individual with a disabling visual impairment that makes it extremely difficult to see in dim lighting applies for a position as a waiter in a nightclub and requests that the club be brightly lit as a reasonable accommodation. Although the individual may be able to perform the job in bright lighting, the nightclub will probably be able to demonstrate that that particular accommodation, though inexpensive, would impose an undue hardship if the bright lighting would destroy the ambience of the nightclub.

The key phrase here is "will probably." For businesses prosecuted under this section, their trials are pure Kafka: they can't be told what law they have broken because the law won't be made until the judge hands down his decision.

In practicing this back-stage management Congress employs a number of strategies to control agency decisions. Reg negs and confrontational hearings are two. Committee and conference reports are another. The reports that committees issue along with bills cannot be amended on the House or Senate floor as the actual legislation can. For this reason committee reports are a favorite place to stash pork projects or favors to interest groups: items that might not survive if they had to be voted on.

Reports also give Congress a head start on influencing regulatory decisions. By the time legislation comes out of the conference committees that try to reconcile House and Senate versions of a bill, the language is usually so convoluted that almost no one, not even the sponsors of the bill, let alone the conferees who voted on it, know everything that is in it. The compromise language is put together by staffers, who are notorious for throwing in little changes that their bosses never notice. For those lawmakers who want some clue as to what they are voting on, a conference report outlines the legislation. Written by the majority staff, conference reports also give Democrats, who currently hold that majority, a chance to put their "spin" on the bill. The legislation might be vague, but the report can explain that the conferees meant for it to be interpreted in a clear and specific way. Not surprisingly, the interpretation given in the conference report is usually that preferred by Democratic staffers.

Now, it might be easy to conclude that Congress is simply incapable of clarity. But when it comes to pork, Congress somehow finds the strength of specificity. Legislators don't want to avoid responsibility for pork; in fact, they want their names pasted all over the projects. When a new traffic interchange or strip of road is at stake, watch how easy it is for Members to get clear and specific. The detail can quickly become ridiculous, such as this item in the Intermodal Surface Transportation Efficiency Act of 1991 (also known as the Highway Bill):

(x) CHAMBERSBURG, PENNSYLVANIA.
— Not later than 30 days after the date of the enactment of this Act, in Chambersburg,

Pennsylvania, at both the intersection of Lincoln Way and Sixth Street and the intersection of Lincoln Way and Coldbrook Avenue, the Pennsylvania Department of Transportation shall include an exclusive pedestrian phase in the existing lighting sequence between the hours of 8:00 and 8:30 a.m. and between the hours of 2:45 and 3:45 p.m. on weekdays.

It is hard to see what business it is of the federal government to be directing the crosswalk signals on Lincoln Way, but at least there won't be a decade of expensive litigation trying to figure out what Congress meant.

The Enforcers on the Hill

One of the most troubling developments in Washington over the last decade has been the criminalization of policy disputes. The Ethics in Government Act, with its strict conflict-of-interest provisions and the menacing presence of that Frankenstein monster, the independent counsel, has become the prime weapon for the enforcers on Capitol Hill. Administration officials who buck Congress increasingly find themselves accused of some conflict of interest, or better yet, the *appearance* of a conflict of interest.

Here's how the game works. A powerful Member of Congress is displeased with an agency official who is responsible for regulations that he doesn't like. So the lawmaker has his committee staff issue subpoenas for any and all agency documents they can get their hands on. Staff attorneys then pore through the files to find any indiscretion by the agency official or his subordinates. The mere appearance of an impropriety will do. The staff often gets help in such fishing expeditions from bureaucrats in the agency who don't like their boss's policies. The official is then called before a congressional hearing where he is accused of any number of crimes. If the official is unrepentant, his sworn testimony is then scrutinized for any misstep or misstatement that can be construed as misleading or lying to Congress. An omission that merely seems to mislead Congress is enough for accusations of perjury. If the official is particularly obstinate, an independent counsel is dispatched, thus burying the offending administrator in a legal catacomb that will take years and millions of dollars to escape.

Congress's delegation of its powers to the federal bureaucracy leaves little legal structure for legislators and the executive to work out their policy differences. The Constitution provides a legal process for the making of law, a process that allows the separate branches to fight over policy without killing one another. If Congress passes a bill the President doesn't like, he can veto it. And if lawmakers can muster the votes, they can override his veto, and he has to live with it. The process makes clear who wins and who loses, and the issue is resolved. Either the bill becomes law or it doesn't. But now, law is largely made, not through the normal legislative process, but through the rulemaking process of the regulatory agencies. And, unlike the lawmaking process, which has a clear end point, regulatory battles go on and on. And even when agency rules have been promulgated they can be changed. In the struggle between Congress and the President to control the crucial making of regulation there is no legal process, and so Congress has turned to policy-inspired prosecutions as a means of getting what it wants. The result is that Congress manages to run the Washington establishment while avoiding any accountability for it.

Congress should legislate, and nothing more. That is its constitutional role, and it is only by abdicating their responsibilities that lawmakers gave birth to the giant administrative state in Washington. If Congress cannot get its way through non-legislative activities, such as bullying hearings, investigations or pressure on bureaucrats — the "micro-management" that conservatives have so long complained of — it will find itself forced to return to its proper role. Demanding that Congress return to its legislative role is not a call for a weakened Congress or an "Imperial" President. If anything, Congress has more power when it exercises its legislative rights. But that power entails responsibility. Unambiguous legislative action can be understood by voters, who are then in a position to hold their representatives accountable. A Congress that is democratically accountable would no longer be a Congress in need of reform.

Who Lost Iraq?

In the summer of 1992, Congress was engaged in a classic set of investigations, looking into whether the Bush administration encouraged Iraq's invasion of Kuwait by favoring Iraq in its war with Iran, and helping Saddam Hussein build up his army. By the spring, with the Presidential election season already in full swing, five different congressional committees were investi-

gating so-called Iraq-gate. Texas Democrat Henry
Gonzalez was using his Banking Committee to investi-
gate loans that the United States guaranteed for Iraq to
purchase American grain. Rep. Charlie Rose, a North
Carolina Democrat, was looking at the same Commod-
ity Credit Corporation (CCC) loan guarantees from the
vantage point of his Agriculture subcommittee. So too
was Vermont Democratic Sen. Patrick Leahy, with his
Agriculture, Nutrition and Forestry Committee. And
Rep. Doug Barnard, a Georgia Democrat, was using his
Subcommittee on Commerce, Consumer, and Monetary
Affairs to determine whether the Commerce Department
was right in allowing Iraq to buy heavy trucks that could
be used for military as well as civilian purposes. These
four legislators appeared in early June as witnesses at a
sort of mega-investigation being held by Texas Democratic
Rep. Jack Brooks, chairman of the House Judiciary
Committee. The four were there to call for the
appointment of (what else?) an independent counsel.

A formal request for an independent counsel can be
made by half of one party's Members on either the House
or Senate Judiciary Committee. The only catch is, they
must specify a criminal offense. Misjudgment in foreign
policy, however egregious, is not criminal. But Members
are not that easily daunted. They fell back on the old
standby: the charge of lying to, or misleading, Congress.
Agriculture Department (USDA) officials involved in
the CCC program had told a congressional committee
that no "undue political pressure" had been placed on the
USDA to authorize the loan guarantees. In truth, the
White House and the State Department had been lob-
bying the USDA to allow the credits, as a way of

supporting the Iraqis in the years before the Gulf War. Whether or not this amounted to "undue" pressure is a judgment call. But the prosecutors on Capitol Hill were in no mood for judgment calls. When Members smell blood, they become a most punctilious lot.

The main weapon in the congressional armory is the charge of "misleading Congress." "Lying to Congress" can be hard to prove. "Misleading" Congress is much easier because all lawmakers have to do is to say they got the wrong impression from some testimony — of course, lawmakers would never fib about what their "impressions" were — and then blame it on the witness. Even when Members really do get the wrong impression, they never ask whether it was their own fault: Legislators often don't understand the answers they are being given because they don't even understand the questions they are asking. At the average hearing, lawmakers are simply reading from cue-cards handed them by their staffs. Nonetheless, the charge of misleading Congress provided one of the bases cited by House Judiciary Committee Democrats in their July 9, 1992, call for an independent counsel to investigate Iraq-gate.

To be sure, some investigation of the administration's tilt toward Iraq was in order. The State Department continued to support Saddam Hussein well after the evidence had piled up about Iraq's ruthless ambitions. Hussein's use of chemical weapons against the Kurds should have been reason enough to abandon efforts to moderate the Hussein regime through grain sales. But such mistakes are not criminal. They may be wrong, and it may be quite proper to criticize such policy flaws. But the proper realm for such disputes is the political, not the legal. If the public agreed that the mistakes made by the administration were crucial, then the voters would be in a position to punish the President by not returning him to office.

Through the criminalization of policy differences, Congress has given the administration good reason to be tight-lipped. When any statement is potential grist for an independent counsel investigation into the misleading of Congress, is it any wonder that administration officials become noncommittal, trying not to say very much at all? We have seen it happen with nominations to the Supreme Court. Since lawmakers have taken to using the statements of nominees as nothing but tools for discrediting them, would-be justices have stopped making statements. Clarence Thomas pretended to have never thought about abortion. David Souter breezed into Washington without a paper trail, never having made much in the way of a statement in his life.

Congress today is a place where prosecution substitutes for legislation, and where the language of justice is misused to eliminate enemies. This noxious habit has poisoned Washington, driving good people out of public life, particularly in the executive branch. But the corruption of the system has also had a deleterious effect on Congress itself. Rather than engaging in serious, and balanced, inquiries into faulty policies, a process that might lead to valuable lessons for the future, Congress reflexively grasps for a hide to nail to the wall. The world's greatest deliberative body has become the world's most infamous accusatory one, and Americans are disgusted with the process at the same time they are transfixed by the flying accusations.

4
OTHER PEOPLE'S MONEY

*I didn't become a United States Senator to sit
around and worry about the fine details.*

—Senate Budget Committee Chairman
James Sasser explaining that he
doesn't like math.

Of all the battles over federal spending, few are
more revealing about congressional mores than the 1992
fight over the Corporation for Public Broadcasting
(CPB). The controversy began as an effort by conservative Republicans to chastise the Public Broadcasting
System (PBS) for airing left-leaning, quasi-pornographic
programs. By the end, the debate had shifted to whether
the federal government should be in the business of
paying for television in the first place. In a time of
staggering budget deficits, the ultimate triumph of those
who argued in favor of shelling out $350 million a year

to air BBC reruns illustrates why reforming congressional spending habits appears next to impossible.

Though only a tiny portion of the federal budget,
public broadcasting illustrates perfectly the division
between the elites who spend and the taxpayers who foot
the bills. Indeed, if ever a federal beneficiary qualified as
a welfare queen, it is public broadcasting. The federal
subsidy accounted for only 17 percent of public radio
and TV budgets in 1992, with the rest coming from
individual, corporate and foundation donations and state
and local governments. More to the point, its viewers are
more than capable of paying their own way. A rate card
sent out by Washington, D.C., public television station
WETA boasted that the average household net worth of
contributors to the station was $627,000. One in seven
WETA contributors had a wine cellar; one in three had
been to Europe within the past three years.

The stations serving such impoverished audiences
receive all manner of government assistance. Take the
Educational Broadcasting Corporation of New York,
which operates the PBS station WNET. In fiscal year
1989, various government agencies gave the corporation grants totalling $30 million. Of this, $16.7 million
came from the federal government via the CPB, $220,000
from the National Science Foundation, $155,000 from
the National Endowment for the Humanities, $116,000
from the National Endowment for the Arts, $69,000
from the National Aeronautics and Space
Administration, and $43,000 from the U.S. Postal
Service. An additional $10 million came from New York
state government agencies and $560,000 from the state
of New Jersey.

The Educational Broadcasting Corporation used these funds to pay their staff members lavish salaries. In the 1989-90 fiscal year, WNET Executive Producer Lester Crystal received salary and benefits of over $400,000; President Trustee William F. Baker received $275,000 in salary and benefits; and George Page, executive producer and host of the "Nature" series, received $240,000 in benefits and salary. At least 12 other WNET officials received six-figure compensation packages. William W. Whaley, Divisional President of the Children's Television Workshop, received $641,224 in salary and benefits in 1991.

During the debate over PBS funding, columnist George Will questioned the propriety of taking money from working people to subsidize the pleasures of the upper middle class. In the Senate, Republican Leader Robert Dole argued that public broadcasting subsidies are a luxury that the nation cannot afford in hard times.

In the end, however, only 11 Senators voted even to limit spending increases for PBS. The lop-sided vote for this pork-for-the-well-heeled bill suggests why it is so hard to cut spending. As with every other item on the federal budget, public broadcasting has a constituency, one that is made up of everyone who watches the *McNeil/Lehrer Newshour* or *Masterpiece Theatre*. This audience enjoys public radio and television, and they aren't about to see its subside cut back without raising a fuss. They are joined by a second constituency: all those for whom public broadcasting represents a job. These people have the most reason to mobilize in defense of the public broadcasting budget, and mobilize they did.

Against this the vast body of taxpayers who neither work for public broadcasting nor enjoy its programming remained virtually silent. A few people offended by PBS documentaries celebrating such things as the lesbian and gay counter-culture did get involved. But their reasons were ideological rather than financial. Taxpayers as a group were not heard.

Not that this was much of a surprise. The entire public broadcasting bill added up to $1.1 billion over three years. A lot of money, yes, but divide it among the 112 million taxpayers in the country, and its elimination would save the average taxpayer only $3.27 a year.

This is the age-old dilemma of special interest spending: The benefits flowing from the spending are focused, while the costs are spread out. It is the beneficiaries, then, who always win the day. Take a penny from each taxpayer, and none will notice it. Give that million dollars to one person, however, and he will most certainly notice it. Conversely, give taxpayers back their pennies and again they won't notice. But take away the beneficiary's million dollar present and his hollering will be heard for miles.

Nearly every congressional spending program operates the same way. Each taxpayer shares the costs; a select group reaps the benefits. And it is the beneficiaries who nearly always dominate the debates. When the question is subsidies to Amtrak, rail employees and passengers make their way to the mikes. When the question is farm subsidies, farmers. Art subsidies, artists. If given a chance, taxpayers might opt to reduce their taxes as a whole by setting the total spending level first. That was the idea behind the Budget Act of 1974. But the Budget Act had few real impediments to spending, and Congress does everything it can to ignore even those.

The Tragedy of the Commons

For centuries, English farmers grazed their cattle on public pastures called "commons." They were good farmers but repeatedly put too many animals in the commons. The land was overgrazed and cows as a result weighed less, gave less milk, and were prone to disease. The farmers knew this but kept doing it. Why?

Pasturage on commons is free except for each farmer's share of the upkeep, so he can raise his cows there more cheaply. His share of the upkeep remains the same no matter how many cows he has, so his incentive is to pasture as many as possible. The more cows, the lower his unit cost and the greater his profit. Everyone else does the same despite the overgrazing and reduced milk and meat.

The same is true for any publicly owned, below-market-cost resource held as "commons," such as public fisheries, forests, wild game, minerals, and western grazing land. The incentive is always to overuse the resource, even to its destruction, and in a race by all to do it before someone else does. This exploitation is known to economists as the "Commons Problem" of public ownership. When one can get the benefit and not pay the cost, there is no reason to act with restraint or to conserve the resource for long-term use and profit. For similar reasons, if your party agrees to split the dinner tab equally, everyone has a mischievous incentive to order the most expensive food. Again, benefit is divorced from cost.

Federal spending is just such a dinner. We are gorging ourselves because not one of us has been asked to pay his own tab. So the shouts for more and more services escalate and Congress is happy to play along. The logic of the commons is such that by handing out money, Congressmen earn the focused gratitude of beneficiaries, while the distress of taxpayers is fragmented. Most taxpayers would be willing to forego pork if everyone else did the same. But as long as local spending is funneled through Washington, no one complains when his Congressman brings the bacon home. Naturally Members of Congress relish the electoral gratitude that comes with this job. So they perpetuate a federal commons.

To make sure legislators get full credit, Congress has structured spending so that they can get their pictures taken handing out the checks. Consider what has happened to federal highway spending. The bill that authorized the interstate highway system, the Federal-Aid Highway Act of 1956, was just 32 pages long. Compare that with the highway bill Congress crafted in 1991, the Intermodal Surface Transportation Efficiency Act. In addition to the 298 pages of small-print text in the bill itself, the accompanying conference report goes on for another 186 pages.

Packed into the bill is project after project of pork amounting to billions. Each Member was happy to sign off on the total bill, as long as he knew his own project would be included. Indeed, such was their zeal to take credit that Members insisted their names or those of their relatives and patrons be placed on these projects. Section 1083 of part A, for example, declared a Pennsylvania highway to be the "J. Clifford Naugle Bypass" and a lock and dam on Louisiana's Red River the "Lindy Claiborne Boggs Lock and Dam." Section

1083(d)(1) of the bill declared "the boat ramp constructed on the left bank of the Mississippi River at River Mile 752.5 at Shelby Forest in Shelby County, Tennessee, shall be known and designated as the 'Joseph Ralph Sasser Boat Ramp,'" in honor of Democratic Sen. James Sasser's father.

Defenders of pork argue that it is just a way for taxpayers to get back the money they send to Washington. But one should not be grateful just to get back what ought to have been one's own money all along, especially after it has been laundered through the Washington spending machine. It would be akin to describing an income tax refund as a gift from the government.

There are two main problems with Congress as the nation's spending middleman. The first is, sending tax dollars to Washington and then having them sent back is profoundly inefficient. There is the cost of federal tax collection; the cost of the federal bureaucracy; the cost of complying with federal paperwork; the cost of navigating red tape; the costs associated with lost flexibility; and the cost of delay. In other words, doing business with Washington is ruinous because of the federal government's overhead.

The second, and more important, reason to resist funneling money through Washington is the fact that it is by controlling money that Congress exercises its greatest powers. Handing our money over to Washington then asking for it back is rather like turning our bank accounts into a trust fund, and asking Congress to give us money only when Members deem it in our best interest. Free citizens should shudder at the thought of such a paternalistic arrangement. And even if we didn't

feel competent to govern ourselves, would we want to
entrust such powers to Congress?

The Shell Game

Along with other tricks, Congress has perfected the
phony spending cut. The most pervasive — and cynical
— tool for making phony cuts is something known as the
"current services baseline." When lawmakers pass an
appropriation bill and pat themselves on the back for
cutting spending, chances are Congress has just spent
more than it did the year before. How can Congress
spend more and yet claim that it has cut spending? The
spending level legislators use to match their new bills
against (the "baseline") is not the amount that was spent
the previous year. Instead, they project automatic annual
increases in every program for inflation, population
growth, and other factors. These estimates are routinely,
and purposefully, high. When the real bill is completed,
therefore, it is likely to be less expensive than the bogus
bill estimated in the current services budget. A cut, then,
is when Congress doesn't spend as much more money as
it thought it might.

Between the political incentives to increase spending,
and Congress's bag of tricks, cutting the budget will not
be easy, especially in the area of entitlements, where
increases are triggered automatically. Putting the burden
of proof on cost-cutters means entitlement programs
will rarely be slowed. But, if welfare and other entitlement programs had to be funded anew every two or five
years, they would have to be defended. This would at
least give the advocates of savings a chance.

To be successful, the advocates of savings have to be more far-reaching. Primarily this means eliminating programs outright rather than simply cutting them back. As long as a program remains in existence, the constituencies for that program will continue to lobby for more spending. The public broadcasting subsidy, which was cut under Reagan, is a perfect example.

Still, until Congress reforms its budget process there will be no stomach for cutting programs. To break the logic of the commons, a real budget total must be set each year. If the total amount the federal government is going to spend is determined first (as many states and virtually all households do), only then to be followed by how much will be allocated to each program, the advocates of savings might have a chance to make themselves heard. Taxpayers would have an incentive to get involved if their *overall* tax bill was at stake, rather than, for example, a $112-million special interest appropriation that only costs each of the 112 million taxpayers in the country one dollar.

5

THE REELECTION MACHINE

I have to be — you heard of a whore? I'm a whore. I am a political whore. And I'm going to play it to the hilt... Shaking hands and kissing everybody. I mean I'm here to get elected.

I'll be going to a lot of funeral homes. Just walk in and — if I faintly remember who these people are — just walk in and shed a little tear and sign my name and take off.

—Former Rep. Joe Kolter explaining his election strategy to his staff.

Going into her 1992 primary, Rep. Mary Rose Oakar found herself in a good deal of trouble. First there were the 213 rubber checks that ranked the Ohio Democrat as one of the top 22 abusers of the House Bank. Then she had to withdraw from an investigation of drug sales and money-laundering at the House Post Office because she herself faced charges (later refuted) of sponsoring ghost employees. Facing serious competition for the first time in years, Oakar didn't address the scandals she was implicated in. Instead, she ran television ads heralding the constituent services she has provided her district. In one, Cleveland residents were paraded across the screen to tell how Oakar helped them when they were in need. At the end of the spot a crowd is gathered around Oakar while a voice announces that she deserves to be returned to office as a payback for all these good works.

The reliance on constituent service apparently did the trick — in a crowded primary field, Mary Rose Oakar received a plurality of 39 percent. It was evident from her commercials that Oakar thought casework was her strongest card. Noted congressional scholar Morris Fiorina estimates that 5 to 10 percent of an incumbent's vote-total can be attributed to gratitude for constituent services. For Oakar, casework made the crucial difference. However, she was defeated in the general election.

So popular is the practice of doing favors for constituents, that lawmakers use it as an excuse for almost everything. When Sen. John McCain of Arizona was accused of using his influence with federal regulators on behalf of constituent (and campaign contributor) Charles Keating, he wrapped himself in the armor of Social Security. "I have done this kind of thing many, many times," said McCain, the only Republican member of the Keating five. What he did for Keating was no different than "helping the little lady who didn't get her Social Security."

Actually, McCain — who was ultimately cleared of any wrong-doing — was telling the truth. Helping constituents has become the primary reelection strategy, involving everything from clearing a path with federal, state, or local regulators to firing up the pilot light in the kitchen when it goes out.

An errand boy for his district, the average legislator builds up a base of nonpartisan goodwill that puts him out of range of most any challenger. Charles Keating's campaign contributions obviously did buy him some special attention, but McCain would probably have gone to bat for Keating even had the banker not given him mounds of money. Such constituent service is even more important to reelection than campaign cash. And, inasmuch as Keating was a large employer in McCain's state, helping him amounted to helping hundreds or even thousands of voters.

When the guffaws got too loud McCain did finally switch from the Little-Old-Lady's-Social-Security-Check to the Mistakes-Were-Made tack. But the other half of Arizona's Senate delegation, Democrat Dennis DeConcini, never did. DeConcini was perceived as the ringleader in the Keating affair: The key meeting between Senators and regulators who were investigating Keating was held in DeConcini's office, and he persisted in accusing the regulators of trying to put Keating out of business. Unlike McCain (who had backed off when regulators told him Keating might be engaged in criminal fraud), DeConcini could not get away with a simple apology. So he turned to constituent service with a vengeance.

As the Keating scandal ripened in 1989, DeConcini's State Director, Mike Crusa, said his boss's record of constituent service would "stand him in good stead." If voters punished him for intervening on Keating's behalf, then lawmakers would shy away from constituent service. In other words: If voters want someone around to take care of glitches in their disability or Medicaid payments, they'd better treat DeConcini with kid gloves:

> I hope [the Keating affair] does not have a negative impact on what I think is the most valuable resource or role that an elected official plays, and that's working in constituent services. Constituent services is what elected officials are all about, whether it's VA checks, whether it's the fact you can't get your Social Security on time, or your city needs help with federal funding allocations for a needed highway. That's what elected officials are supposed to be for — to mitigate problems with the federal government, with regulators, quite frankly. Regulators have discretion. I hope that this doesn't [reduce constituent service] and I don't think it will, because legitimate constituent services — like Dennis was doing in this particular case — shouldn't be affected by this kind of thing.

Thus has constituent service become a cure-all for incumbents; even when it gets them into trouble, it offers the way out.

Death of the Competitive District

It wasn't always this way. Until the 1930s few citizens had much direct contact with Washington, and even fewer needed help coping with the feds. What changed all this was the New Deal; with the creation of Social

Security, after all, came the little old lady with the missing Social Security check. With each new federal program, new carrots and new sticks have encouraged voters to appeal to their Congressmen. The carrots are the grants federal agencies hand out; the sticks are regulations wielded clumsily by a creaking bureaucratic machine. Congressmen have neatly positioned themselves as the only ones able to stay the blows, even while clearing the way to the grant trough.

What makes it all so beautiful is how it plays on popular sentiment. No one likes a bureaucrat. Drivers don't return to their local Division of Motor Vehicles because of customer satisfaction, after all, so there is no incentive to make the experience a pleasurable one. "We don't care, because we don't have to," goes the joke. Even bureaucracies staffed with the kindest and most accommodating workers tend to be infuriating. Every decision must run through labyrinthine channels, each to be navigated in triplicate.

For Members of Congress, by contrast, customer satisfaction is everything. Legislators have become political entrepreneurs, and they have found their most lucrative market niche in providing fix-it services to those whose encounters with the bureaucracy have been unpleasant, which means just about everyone.

Constituent service started picking up in the 1950s, when the burgeoning bureaucracy began to produce "clients." As the federal government blossomed like so much kudzu, more and more lawmakers found their constituents complaining about their treatment by Washington. By the 1960s a trend had emerged: Legislators who engaged in aggressive constituent service earned the gratitude of voters and were far more likely to get reelected than those who didn't. By the 1970s that trend had become a racket. More than anything else — more than PAC money to incumbents, more than the disproportionate amount of advertising that money buys — this institutionalization of constituent service has killed competition in congressional races.

Political scientists David Mayhew and Morris Fiorina recognized this critical relationship between constituent service and incumbency early on. Mayhew pointed out that in the early 1970s, not only were incumbents winning reelection more often, they were winning by larger margins. Ever rarer were the so-called marginal districts, where the winner gained less than 55% of the vote. If the winner's victory is narrow, he is more likely to be vulnerable the next time around. Conversely, if the winning percentage is high (60 percent or more) even widespread voter dissatisfaction probably won't be enough to dethrone an incumbent.

Mayhew offered several explanations for why marginal districts were disappearing, mainly that franked mail and pork-barrel politics helped incumbents boost their popularity. But Fiorina recognized that it is constituent service that makes the difference. As we have seen, lawmakers avoid taking politically sensitive stands. Indeed, Congress avoids making decisions at all, delegating tough choices to the federal agencies. Yet, while votes can be politically dangerous, finding Social Security checks is not. Fiorina explains:

> For every voter a Congressman pleases by
> a policy stand he will displease someone else.
> The consequence is a marginal district. But if

we have incumbents who de-emphasize
controversial policy positions and instead
place heavy emphasis on nonpartisan, non-
programmatic constituency service (for
which demand grows as government
expands), the resulting blurring of political
friends and enemies is sufficient to shift the
district out of the marginal camp. We do not
need to postulate a Congressman who is more
interested in reelection today than previously.
All we need postulate is a Congressman
sufficiently interested in reelection that he
would rather be elected as an errand boy than
not be elected at all.

The shift in staff assignments confirms the trend. In
the 1950s the vast majority of Members of Congress had
only one district office, an office that was likely to be
open only when the Member was home, or no district
office at all. But as legislators started to realize that
reelection could be all but assured by solving constituents' problems, they started franchising district offices
faster than McDonald's. By 1987, two-thirds of new
Members of the House set up two or more full-time
district offices. More than 40 percent had at least three
district shops.

Manning these constituent service shops is a small army
of caseworkers. The argument for creating new staff jobs
was that Congress needs to match the analytic skills and
resources of the executive branch, but staffing practice
is another matter altogether. The thousands of new
staffers have not been put to work at legislative analysis;
they have been hired as constituent-service case-

workers. As the number of staff has increased, so has the proportion of the staff assigned to district offices. In 1972, an eighth of Senate staff and less than a quarter of House workers were based in the home state. By 1990, more than a third of Senate staff worked in district offices, as did more than 40 percent of those on the House side. In the last 20 years, Congress has added at least 3,000 new constituent-service jobs to the Capitol Hill payroll.

Since much of the time of Washington-based congressional staff also is spent dealing with voters' problems, it is no exaggeration to say that well over half, and perhaps as much as two-thirds, of congressional staff is engaged in constituent service.

Each of these staffers amounts to a full-time campaign worker, who salary is remitted by the taxpayers. No wonder incumbents have an edge.

For Incumbents Only

The bipartisan cynicism with which this power is used to get reelected is on display in two handbooks for Members of Congress prepared by the Congressional Management Foundation (CMF) and endorsed by both Speaker of the House Thomas Foley and House Minority Leader Robert Michel. The first of the two books, *Setting Course: A Congressional Management Guide,* is addressed to new Members. In addition to general advice (such as, that the Member-elect should get to know his new colleagues), the manual offers specific suggestions. The meat is found under the heading "Creating a First-Term Plan," which has two subheadings, "Choosing Legislative Goals" and "Choosing

Constituent Service Goals." The advice on choosing a legislative strategy is fairly straightforward: the Member-elect should go with the issues that either he or his constituents care about, which his committee assignments allow him to pursue, and which will get him some play in the newspapers and on television.

But the more-detailed information is reserved for choosing a constituent-service strategy. First, the new Member is advised to do basic market research to identify the needs of his clients.

> For example, a Florida Member with heavy concentrations of senior citizens in her district might structure the casework staff to respond to their particular requests (e.g. Social Security benefits)... Similarly, a New York City Member might focus on techniques to address housing problems and a Colorado Member might offer assistance on water supply needs.

The *Congressional Management Guide* also advises Members how to keep others from cutting in on their constituent-service turf, or at least how to choose a niche without competitors vying for the credit:

> Who else is presently serving your constituents in this area? Are state legislators, county government agencies, voluntary organizations, or other entities already addressing the community's needs in an area in which you would like to be proactive? If other entities are already involved in such casework, will it be difficult for you to receive proper credit for your successful efforts?

Displayed here is all the cynicism of the constituent-service scam. The Member of Congress who is the least bit interested in the well-being of his constituents would be happy to learn that their needs were being met by other levels of government or by charitable organizations. In this case the concern would be not to duplicate efforts but to look for areas where no helpers are now working.

The problem for new arrivals to Washington is that these other areas probably lack the electoral payoff that finding Social Security checks has. The real concern, as the manual points out, is not that efforts will be duplicated and thus wasted, but that somebody other than the lawmaker might get the "proper credit."

This is not to say that Members of Congress do not take satisfaction from helping their constituents. Helping constituents is one activity for which they (with exceptions such as the Keating Five) get no grief. Casework is non-controversial, indeed, almost philanthropic. The irony is that the prime reelection vehicle appears selfless. Lawmakers get to pass out favors like Boss Tweed, and feel like Mother Teresa for doing so.

So developed is the effort that lawmakers do not wait for business to come to them, they go out and beat the pavement for new clients. "Members love creating constituent-service work for themselves — much of it not legitimate," said the late Rep. Ned Patterson, a Democrat from New York. Once again, the *Congressional Management Guide* is appallingly exact in its advice. "A constituency-oriented Member," it says, "might conduct outreach mailings to generate additional casework....This might also require adding caseworkers, or recruiting volunteers, and training them to help resolve the additional casework generated by the targeted mailings."

So popular did this guide prove that the CMF followed it with a sequel devoted exclusively to constituent-service operations. *Frontline Management: A Guide for Congressional District/State Offices* has a host of suggestions.

The first is that the Member go home to his district as frequently as possible; the most effective casework is that which appears to have been handled by the Member himself. Once upon a time legislators would go home only during recesses, but now Members travel to their district nearly every weekend. On the surface this may seem like a good idea. How better, after all, to keep legislators in touch with their voters. This assumes, however, that Members are home to find out their constituents' views on the issues of the day. But that is what polls are for. Instead, legislators are in the district to drum up casework and get their faces in front of the voters.

Members used to be limited in the number of round-trip tickets to and from Washington that they could put up on the federal tab. But in 1978 the travel budget was freed of any restrictions as travel, mail, office supplies, and other such expenses were consolidated into one office budget which each Member may use as he sees fit. Most Members see fit to fully fund their casework campaign stops. And not least of the perks that flow from taxpayer-funded travel are frequent-flyer miles that are used for personal trips.

The constant travel is facilitated by even more perks. For example, lawmakers enjoy free parking at Washington's National Airport in a lot that is not only reserved, but which is the closest to the terminal, a great convenience when you're parking at the airport for four days of every week. The weekends are four days long for Members because the legislative schedule has been adapted to fit their casework needs. Except for the end of the year crunch, when lawmakers try to fit the legislative duties they ignored all year into a few weeks, the congressional work-week runs Tuesday through Thursday. It was not until July of 1992, that Senate Majority Leader George Mitchell announced with great fanfare that the Senate would henceforth work five days a week! Two extended vacations and plans to end work for the year on October 2 left only about nine weeks under the Senate's new arduous schedule, however.

The CMF's casework guide also offers some helpful hints about how to increase business on these visits home. Members are encouraged to install toll-free long-distance numbers so out-of-town constituents can call for help without charge. The guide also suggests lawmakers deploy "mobile offices," like constituent-service bookmobiles, to "allow caseworkers to reach constituents who don't live or work near any of the member's district/state offices." The vans serve the added function of mobile billboards, as most have the officeholder's name emblazoned in huge letters on the side.

High on the manual's list, of course, is the use of mass mailings. Much has been said about how the franked newsletters with which Members bombard their districts work as an incumbency advantage: They allow Members to keep their names and faces in front of an electorate that votes in large part on the basis of name recognition. But this analysis misses one of the main purposes for the mailings, which is to advertise constituent services. The ads are usually put where the client can't help but see them, right next to the address on the front of the folded mailing. Rep. Jim Moran's newsletters, for example, are emblazoned with the Virginia Democrat's name and the slogan, "We Are Here to Help You," right above the address for his "Constituent Services" office.

"Any Member who has any trouble puts everything else aside and makes constituent service his only job," says former Rep. Vin Weber, a Minnesota Republican. Constituent service is rolled out when Members feel the heat, which is why those who bounced the most checks at the House Bank have been those most keen to provide services this election cycle.

Because casework is so productive of votes, lawmakers are equal-opportunity suppliers of constituent service. Supplicants do not have to be campaign contributors, or members of the legislator's political party, or even registered voters. Casework is fastidiously nonpartisan because its purpose is to render partisan politics unimportant in elections. In the wake of Watergate, for example, dozens of liberal Democrats were elected in heavily Republican districts. Once the revolutionary fervor of 1974 died down, these new Members recognized that they would not be able to hang on if future contests revolved around their voting records. And so those elected on a platform of reform dropped their snouts in the constituency-service trough. They've been there ever since.

If there is anything more important than constituent service, it's getting credit for it. Channeling federal grants is a good example. As we might expect, the CMF's casework manual offers some sound advice here. "Remember that the constituent is your client," it reads.

"Therefore, it's important that they hear from you if an award is about to be made. This not only reinforces your relationship with the constituent, but reminds him of the instrumental role your office played in obtaining the grant — a point you would like them to remember when reporters call."

The most amusing (and cynical) suggestion is that congressional offices should have letters ready claiming credit even for grants that the Member had nothing to do with. "For awards you're not expecting, make sure you have a standardized procedure to follow so you can still be quick in getting the word out. A grant announcement form with blanks to be filled in means that anyone [in the congressional office] can take the information if you're not available at the time…. A nice touch is to follow up with a congratulatory letter to the recipient." And how does the Member know about a grant to his constituent? A helpful package put together by the (taxpayer-financed) Congressional Research Service gives the answer. Entitled "Grants Work in a Congressional Office" (the cover of which warns that it is for *"CONGRESSIONAL OFFICE USE ONLY"*), the report explains that "the usual announcement procedure in cases of allocated Federal funds is for the agency making the award to notify the Senate office first, the House office, and finally the recipient." This inside information allows Members to make a killing on the credit-claiming market.

Patching Tires or Sweeping Tacks

The most distressing aspect of these arrangements is how they pervert incentives for Members. If lawmakers confined themselves to helping constituents out when they had a legitimate gripe against the government, that would be one thing. But not only are most Members of Congress part of the problem in the first place, they have an incentive to encourage the bureaucracy to injure voters just so they will be made into constituency-service clients. They have become like the owner of a gas station who throws nails on the road in front of his business and then cleans up when motorists must have their flat tires repaired. The drivers, who don't know the full story, do not blame the gas station attendant for their punctured tires. Instead they are grateful he is there to fix their tires so quickly.

The majority of those in Congress are not as overt as this gas station owner. Then again, they don't have to be. They are more like the gas station owner who sees that a box of nails has been spilled on the road. He didn't put them there, and he could easily sweep the street, but he has no incentive to do so. In fact, the business the nails produce provides an incentive to do just the opposite.

There might be more hope that Congress would reform this system were it not for the way the constituent-service scam has affected legislators. When Morris Fiorina identified the casework racket in the 1970s, he expected it to fall apart because people capable enough to become lawmakers "might not be willing to spend their careers as errand boys." But Fiorina has since written off his earlier view as hopeless optimism. Now, he says, the type of people drawn to Capitol Hill are those who don't mind being glorified go-fers.

"Glorified" is the operative word here. Although perks rile the public, and legislators know this, they still court public revolt by perpetuating special privileges. On one level it makes no sense. Why, when so much of their activity is aimed at reducing the risk of offending voters, do Members of Congress wallow in perks bound to annoy these same constituents? Perhaps because privilege gives lawmakers the sense of worth and importance that they have not been able to earn through their meager legislative accomplishments. Lawmakers may be mere errand boys, but they are the only go-fers on earth who never have to pick up their own dry cleaning, walk their own dogs, or drive around looking for a parking space.

Whenever the perks of office become an issue, congressional apologists complain that the public is being silly, that ending perks would not put a dent in the deficit. When really pressed, they point to the perquisites enjoyed by the administration. To begin with, these two arguments are inconsistent: If cutting Hill perks won't balance the budget (and it won't), then neither will cutting the benefits of the executive branch. Beyond that, the argument misses the point because citizens do not think of the President the same way they think of legislators. As President Jimmy Carter found out, a President who downplays the accoutrements of his office comes across as ridiculous. Those in Congress, by contrast, are representatives of the people, and as such should embody the democratic ideals of the nation rather than its power and stature. The self-glorification of Members flies in the face of that democratic idea. The public dislikes congressional perks, not because of what they cost, but because they are the trappings of an Imperial Congress.

This is the lesson of the check-kiting scandal at the House Bank. The public has been chastised again and again for finding Representatives' proclivity for bouncing checks offensive. The bank was not really a bank, we are told. No public money was lost, we are reassured. But those in Congress just don't get it. Voters do not care whether some trivial amount of money was or was not lost at the House Bank. They care that Members got to write checks without worrying whether they could cover them, something no other citizen can do. Voters care that legislators have set themselves up as a privileged class. And the more they find out about Washington's ruling class, the angrier they get.

Nevertheless, in a paradox often noted by pundits, voters manage to like their own particular Member while holding the institution and the rest of its inmates in contempt. The televised talking heads of Washington's political gab shows love this paradox because it lets them chuckle over how clueless the average schmoe is. But the voters are not to blame: In liking their own representatives while disdaining the rest, they are not behaving irrationally. They are simply responding in a sensible way to the incentives of a rigged and fraudulent system.

The Money (non-)Problem

So what can we do? For starters, we should not get distracted by that perennial red herring, campaign-finance reform. Whenever the question of incumbency is raised in Washington, it is pointed out that incumbents on average raise and spend two to three times as much as challengers. To rein in incumbency, the argument goes, we need to put limits on campaign spending, perhaps even initiate public financing of congressional elections.

The problem here is that the enormous inequalities in campaign spending have come about not because of a lack of spending restrictions. They owe themselves to a previous round of reform. In the 1974 election, the last before the Watergate-era reforms that put limits on certain types of campaign fundraising, the average amount spent by House incumbents was $56,539, compared with $40,015 for challengers. Since then, the gap in spending has grown steadily. In 1990, the average challenger spent little more than a fourth of the $399,310 thrown around by the average incumbent. Is there any reason to believe that a new set of finance rules drafted and approved by incumbents would be any fairer to challengers?

Indeed, campaign finance becomes a chicken-or-the-egg dilemma: does money produce incumbency, or incumbency, money? Without doubt, an incumbent's chances are related to how much more money he spends than the challenger. In House races where a Democratic incumbent won with 60 percent or more of the vote in 1990, the incumbent spent on average more than five times the amount spent by the Republican challenger. Spending was much closer in races where the margin of victory for officeholders was under 20 points; there, challengers spent somewhat less than half of the incumbents' total. In those rare instances where office-holders were chucked out (only 15 incumbents lost in 1990), the average challenger spent well over half that spent by his opponent.

But money does not make incumbents. Rather, it is the other way around. Incumbents spend more money because they have more money to spend; they have more money to spend because Political Action Committees (PACs) tend to give more to the candidate they believe will win. And PACs know that the constituent-service racket, and all the perks that make it so effective — franked mailings, free travel, and hordes of casework staff — all but ensure that incumbents will get reelected. This puts officeholders in a position to shake down PACs for all they are worth. The money incumbents get, then, is not the fuel of their reelection machines, it is instead a product of the absurdly high rate of reelection enjoyed by congressional incumbents. The money does, in turn, add to incumbents' success rates, but most likely only marginally. Without PAC money congressional reelection rates might not be as high: Maybe only 95 percent rather than the 98.3 percent it hit in 1988.

Shutting Down the Favor Factory

Given that incumbents are unlikely to write rules that will do themselves serious damage, real reforms are generally those that Members of Congress hate. And more than anything else, legislators hate the idea of term limits.

On no issue are the opinions of lawmakers at greater odds with the views of the electorate than on this subject. Three-quarters or more of Americans see no reason anyone should stay on Capitol Hill for more than 10 or 12 years. Three-quarters of the legislators could not disagree more. The most popular argument made by opponents to term limits is that it would throw out the good with the bad, that talented and dedicated legislators would be lost when their Hill time was up. This line of reasoning assumes, of course, that there will not be an equal number of talented and dedicated citizens eager to take their places. And, even if that assumption were true, the loss of experience would not come close to out-weighing the gains. Take away the possibility of staying forever and legislators would soon tire of playing the role of errand boy.

The solution to the constituent-service racket may ultimately be the same as the answer to the problem of legislative delegation: Force Congress to legislate and nothing more. By removing Capitol Hill's tools of ethics assassination the President would then be able to ignore Congress's non-legislative demands.

Finally, part of the solution rests with us, the voters, who are in a position to reject constituent service. We can let our Representatives and Senators know that we expect them to legislate, not run errands; we can tell them we are not impressed or amused by their publicity-stunt hearings. And, when the power goes out on the weekend, we can call the electrician ourselves rather than ringing our friendly neighborhood lawmaker.

6
REFORM

> *The Congress shall have power ... To make all laws which shall be necessary and proper for carrying into execution the foregoing powers and all other powers vested by this constitution in the Government of the United States....*

Constitution of the United States
Article I, Section 8

To make all laws. When the Founding Fathers divided our government among three distinct branches, the role they intended for Congress was clear: Congress was to legislate. It is no coincidence, then, that problems in Congress are in direct proportion to how far the

---

The reform agenda in this chapter flows not only from the analysis of this book, but also from the policy recommendations developed in writings and working groups of The Heritage Foundation's U.S. Congress Assessment Project, led by David M. Mason.

legislature has moved from its assigned task. Congress-men today prefer to do just about anything *but* legislate. What pass for laws are either vague exhortations em-powering bureaucrats and special interests to fill in the details (the ADA and the Clean Air Act) or self-parody-ing pork (traffic crossings in Chambersburg, Pennsylva-nia). We have seen what Congress does instead, and the results: enthronement of special interests, enervation of the executive, confusion abroad, debasing of political debate, and policy gridlock. Congress prefers this sys-tem because by abandoning legislation, Congressmen escape accountability. Fixing Congress thus requires a return to legislation and the accountability it brings.

Accountability, of course, is essential for citizens to fulfil their responsibilities in a government of, by, and for the people. So long as lawmakers' activities are evident to the public, voters bear responsibility for any resulting faults. Congressional apologists like to pretend that this is in fact what we have: Because Members regularly face the voters and are repeatedly returned to office, they argue, the voters must approve. Reform isn't needed because citizens have it in their power to throw the bums out, as the 1992 turnover in Congress demon-strates. But as John Fund and James Coyne point out in their recent book *Cleaning House,* advocating limits on congressional terms, "Almost all the turnover in 1992 is due to three simple (and simply outrageous) reasons: redistricting, the House Bank scandal, and this year's once-in-a-lifetime campaign fund 'retirement bonus.' How often can voters count on such a political windfall?"

To know whether to throw the bums out, the electorate has to know what the bums have been up to.

And as we have seen again and again, the bums are very good at hiding what they have done. Through procedural sleight of hand, Congressmen make it appear they are doing one thing when they are doing another. Backwards legislating has created an administrative state, shifting the responsibility for making laws onto the shoulders of bureaucrats and setting Congressmen up as monopoly providers of fix-it services for those injured or inconvenienced by the regulators' laws. Capitol Hill hearings allow legislators to confront, interrogate, and accuse without themselves having to take a stand on the issues. Spending is structured so that only those hollering "gimme" are heard. Congressional staff run a shadow government, often unaccountable to even their bosses, not to mention the voters, from whom they are twice removed. And anyone who challenges the system is run out of town by a special prosecutor.

In all these ways, Washington's Ruling Class has perfected the art of grabbing credit while avoiding blame. This — not voter satisfaction — explains why Congressmen are returned to Capitol Hill with such regularity. It also explains why even the hint of scandal is electoral nitroglycerin: Voters know the system is broken, and they will take whatever clues they can find. Check-kiting was not the cause of the legislative morass, but the public assumes, not unreasonably, that those who abused the House Bank may be part of the problem in other respects as well.

Lawmakers know how to write clear and specific laws when they need to — that is, when there is credit to be grabbed. Appropriations bills, stuffed with pork ripe for the picking, have become treatises of infinite legal detail specifying exactly who gets what. But the broadest-reaching legislation, addressing issues such as civil rights and the environment, is either contradictory or, more often, bewilderingly vague. Congress has been reduced to legislating noble sentiments, leaving unelected, unaccountable bureaucrats to hammer those sentiments into the legal specifics that everyone but Congress has to live with. This makes Congress unaccountable as well. Indeed, the more onerous regulations are, the more constituents turn to their representatives for relief. We become supplicants at the foot of Capitol Hill, and in gratitude for whatever balm is applied to our wounds, we reelect the very legislators who allowed the bureaucrats to injure us in the first place.

It's not hard to see why this is bad for America. The rule of law means nothing if the law is different in every place and circumstance, or so vague that you cannot know beforehand what constitutes a violation. It is not much more difficult to see why abandoning legislation is bad for Congress: unaccountability ultimately unravels authority. What is gained in detail and warm feelings is lost in the inability to act decisively on major issues. Details displace larger decisions, issues remain unsettled, interests are at odds, and no one wins in the resulting gang warfare. Legislating forces our representatives to make choices, to take stands, to resolve issues.

Making legislators responsible for the size and shape of the federal government (and making voters aware of that responsibility) not only will reform Congress, it will transform Congress. The only way to make Congressmen accountable in this way is to demand that they return to true legislation. This requires eliminating all the non-legislative powers with which lawmakers have armed themselves. Congress may have delegated most of its legislative duties, but Congressmen still want to be in charge. They use legislative vetoes to trump agency decisions that run contrary to lawmakers' druthers. They fabricate ethics violations to ruin officials who challenge Congress by writing regulations the denizens of Capitol Hill do not like. They cut the budgets of agency offices that do not toe the congressional line. They make special-interest allies part of the rule-making process through regulation negotiations. Take away these and other powers that allow Congressmen to direct the making of regulations and lawmakers will think twice about delegating their legislative authority.

Reforms that would restore Congress's legislative powers would also help the executive branch do its job better. This is not to argue in favor of replacing an imperial Congress with an imperial presidency. If Congress knows it is actually giving up its powers when it delegates, the President may very well end up with less power as the legislature turns to writing real laws. Ending its non-legislative activities, then, would increase rather than reduce Congress's power and authority.

As pointed out in Chapter Three, restoring the constitutional distinction between legislating and executing the laws is also a recipe for ending policy gridlock: real legislation produces final decisions rather than initiating regulatory squabbles. And final decisions will make Congress (and the President) accountable.

To be sure, effecting these reforms is just as important as deciding what reforms to effect. For the most part the necessary reforms are structural: constitutional or other changes external to Congress. This means that public pressure, through the ballot box and otherwise, is critical. It also means that reform is possible; incumbent Congressmen don't hold all the keys. The President can help by organizing his administration to counterbalance legislative overreaching, and leading a public battle for congressional reform. Accountability can also be promoted through internal, procedural reforms to make the legislative process more fair and transparent. Once Congress is accountable, the burden will be on us, the voters, to decide whether we approve of the laws being made. And if we don't, we'll know whom to send packing.

Earlier chapters touched on a number of structural and procedural reforms that will put the law-writing quill back into the hands of Congressmen. These suggestions, designed to make legislators legislate, draw upon the lessons and examples contained in this book to present a comprehensive agenda for reforming Capitol Hill.

Limit Terms. Legislators like pork because it helps them get reelected. They are interested in administrative details because long tenure promotes narrow specialization. The constituent service racket allows lawmakers to ignore big problems by fixing small ones. In becoming ombudsmen — glorified errand boys,— incumbents build up enough good will for most to survive even a watershed year like 1992. By ending congressional careerism, term limits will encourage attention to larger legislative issues. By changing the understanding of the legislator's role, term limits are probably the most effective single reform that can be imposed on Congress. And imposed it will have to be: While great majorities of the American people support term limits, lawmakers oppose them in even larger proportions.

With a career Congress, voters face a dilemma: They do not like paying taxes to Washington and hoping to get them back in the form of pork and entitlements, but as long as the system is rigged, it makes sense to vote for the incumbent to maximize your own take. Congressmen face a similar dilemma: Take the easy road to reelection or face the often difficult choices of balancing local and national interests. Take away the career mindset and both representatives and voters can make choices based on philosophy and the merits of each case.

Ideally, legislators in a democracy are not professionals, but, as Olympic athletes of yore, skilled amateurs. They must be somewhat detached from governing and far more a part of the communities they represent. They must feel a stake in returning, not only to where they once lived, but to what they once did for a living. Even if term limits result only in a cadre of politicians rotating amongst state, local, and federal offices, limiting tenure in Washington would help maintain links between legislators and the communities they represent.

Career incumbents claim that the amateurs sent to Congress as part-timers would have the wool pulled over their eyes by the Washington establishment. That might happen occasionally, though probably not as often as the insiders would have you believe. In fact, one of the biggest benefits of non-professional legislators is that they would be unlikely to join with the bureaucrats and special interests in blowing smoke at the voters.

Given the historic congressional turnover of 1992, some ask whether term limits are moot: Haven't we already thrown the bums out? Despite the turnover, more than two-thirds of the House and an even higher percentage of Senators are returning. Twenty-, thirty-, and even fourty-year incumbents remain in key positions where they can frustrate reform and tame the reformers. More important, unless incentives change, new Members will be lured, some slowly and some more quickly, into the paths that have produced today's problems. Even before they take office, the new representatives elected on a reform platform will be admonished to study the constituent service handbook. Under the current corrupt system those who do so are likely to stay while those who devote their energies to ultimately more important topics run a far higher risk of not being reelected. Thus, the time servers endure, and all too many of the idealists leave. Certainly a few skilled and visionary leaders will be sent home with the rest under term limits, but that is a tiny price compared to the benefits of government by citizen-legislators rather than a ruling class of overrated errand boys.

Limit Sessions. Term limits may not be enough. The number of workdays spent in Washington is as damaging as the number of years in office. Alan Ehrenhalt diagnosed the problem in *The United States of Ambition:* As legislating becomes a full time job, citizen-legislators, who must tend to other careers, are driven out of public life by professional politicians, for whom office-holding is a career. Better representation, and better representatives, will result if Congressmen return for some time each year to their own communities and occupations, not as caseworkers or campaigners but as colleagues of their constituents.

It might be objected that Congress gets too little done as it is, that legislators should earn their keep. It was not until July of 1992, after a year and a half of three-day work weeks (interrupted by some long vacations), that the 102nd Congress went on a five-day schedule. Owing to the urgent press of business, congressional leaders explained, they would work full time for nine whole weeks before going home to campaign. Congress should replace three-day weeks with a five-day schedule, and compress their year-round sessions into six months of honest work. A definite end to sessions will also communicate to Congressmen that they are representatives rather than managers of the permanent bureaucracy.

Cut Staff. There is a staff infection on Capitol Hill, a shadow government of unelected, unaccountable pseudo-legislators. As a panacea for congressional ills, staff cuts rank just behind term limits. Reducing the size of the staff would have productive effects in just about every area: reducing incumbent electoral advantages; trimming the length and complexity of legislation (and encouraging legislators to read it); cutting the volume of midnight deals in conference sessions and committee reports; limiting improper interference with regulatory and other executive branch functions. With fewer aides, lawmakers would have to do more legislative work themselves. They might even go so far as to read bills before voting on them.

To make a real difference the cuts need to be large. In the November presidential elections, Bill Clinton proposed a 25 percent cut in congressional staff, and George Bush offered to slash a third of Capitol Hill's workforce, with an equal percentage of his own aides. But even those numbers are probably not enough. House Republicans have proposed a 50 percent cut in committee staff: a palatable proposal for them since they are dramatically short-changed in committee staff allocations anyway. The problem with the GOP proposal is that committee aides represent only 10 percent of all congressional employees. Cutting the House numbers in half would reduce the overall congressional payroll a paltry 3 percent.

Besides, committee staffers actually help with legislation part of the time. Serious reform requires across-the-board cuts, including personal staff, to force Congress to reassess how it operates and change its behavior. Staff should be cut by at least 25 percent immediately and eventually by 50 percent. Anything less won't be enough to change the way Congressmen conduct casework or micromanage executive agencies.

Limiting terms, limiting the length of Congress's yearly sessions and limiting the number (and the tenure as well) of staffers are all parts of a package. Any one of the three can be implemented with success, but for the legislature to be wrested from the ruling class and returned to the hands of the citizenry, all three must be in effect.

Limit Spending and Balance the Budget. A constitutional amendment is the only way to bring discipline to congressional spending. The 1974 Budget Act, which governs congressional budget decisions, has proven to be a machine to increase spending rather than a tool to control it. The Budget Act consists primarily of internal congressional rules, rather than statutes, so the few restrictions that do exist can be violated at will. Most notably, the annual Congressional Budget Resolution is not a law (and thus cannot be vetoed or signed by the President), making the budget process Congress's most outrageous non-legislative exercise. The result is that spending decisions are made on a case-by-case basis, only the advocates are heard, and too many cows end up on the commons.

Setting a spending level first, and then dividing up the pie would solve this problem. A constitutional amendment would force Congress to do just that. It is by no means impossible to design a system which either automatically limits spending or forces Congress to make difficult decisions. In fact, two different versions of Gramm-Rudman (which altered the 1974 Budget Act) were quite effective; but when the limits began to pinch, Congress just changed the rules. The most flawed of those changes, made in the 1990 budget deal, reinforced the "current services baseline" system of automatic spending increases: No votes are required. Indeed, any limitation in the growth of these bureaucratic wish lists is advertised as a spending "cut."

Most of the arguments against a balanced budget amendment just don't wash. We are told, for instance, that the ratification and phase-in period simply postpones action to balance the budget. This argument might have some merit if Congress were making progress in that direction, but aside from Gramm-Rudman nothing has worked even to limit deficit growth in the last twenty years. Others predict dire consequences when Congress is forced to choose between huge tax increases and draconian spending cuts. This is a congressional version of the "Washington Monument ploy": politically popular programs are the first offered for cuts.

Voters do not object to a choice between spending cuts and tax increases. It is Congressmen, who would have to make such decisions and then be held responsible, who find the alternatives daunting. That 49 states have workable balanced budget provisions renders laughable the arguments that this just cannot be done at the federal level. From time to time, those state requirements have forced unpleasant choices, but nowhere has it proved impossible to live with such budget discipline.

To make a balanced budget amendment honest, however, there must be no automatic tax increase provision — an idea the House Democratic Leadership proposed when the amendment came up for a vote in the spring of 1992. Automatic taxes would make a mockery of any spending limit. Given the choice between voting to cut spending (and taking the heat) and failing to act, thereby triggering an "automatic" tax increase which each legislator can disavow individually, Congress will go for the tax increase every time. We have already seen the results of similar automatic non-votes, under House Rule XLIX, to increase the debt ceiling.

Given the congressional proclivity for higher spending, a balanced budget amendment needs a tax provision that cuts in the opposite direction, making it harder to raise taxes. Wisconsin Republican Sen. Bob Kasten and Texas Republican Rep. Tom DeLay, for instance, have proposed a balanced budget amendment which includes a requirement that any tax increase be approved by a 60 percent majority. Raising the barrier for increasing taxes will make it more difficult to assemble a coalition of spending advocates to provide political cover for new tax schemes.

Like the 60 percent tax requirement, other procedures to enforce a balanced budget amendment should require votes and real legislation rather than automatic devices, which encourage legislative stalemate. If a failsafe mechanism is necessary, it should be in the President's hands, which would provide a strong inducement for Congress to legislate rather than abdicate.

Enhance the President's Role in Setting the Budget. Today the President submits a budget to Congress and has no more to say about overall taxing and spending levels. Making the Concurrent Budget Resolution, which sets those targets, subject to Presidential approval or veto would probably result in lower overall spending and taxation levels. The President's national constituency lends itself more to those broad concerns than to interest in individual programs. Further, setting spending targets by statute would make it far more difficult for Congress to circumvent the limits. Doing so would require a change in the law, signalling the public the budget was about to be busted, and giving the President an opportunity to veto the increases. Coupled with a statutory budget resolution, the President's authority to withhold ("impound") spending in excess of established limits should be restored. These reforms could follow or precede a balanced budget amendment.

Allow a Line-Item Veto. A Presidential line-item veto would help limit spending, though it is far less helpful in this regard than a balanced budget amendment. (Unfortunately Presidents are little more willing than Congress to take the heat for necessary but unpleasant spending cuts.) More importantly, an item veto would allow the President to limit unreasonable congressional encroachments on executive authority, and would enable him to excise pork and other crooked deals concocted by committee chairmen, or even staffers, against the will of the congressional majority. This would greatly limit the degree to which conference committees, for instance, could be abused to approve unpopular provisions in unaccountable secrecy.

While the Founding Fathers did not write an item veto into the Constitution, obviously they did not contemplate the huge and complex omnibus bills that have become so common today. Neither does an item veto equal unlimited executive power. Knowing that their bills were subject to challenge, piece-by-piece, lawmakers would no longer paste bewilderingly large bills together with pork. Instead they would perfect simpler, clearer statutes that could not be pried apart with such a veto. Again, state experience is instructive. Governors in 43 states have item vetoes, which are exercised without irreparable harm to the balance of power between the executive and the legislature.

Make Congress Obey the Laws. Congress exempts itself, actually or effectively, from most civil rights, worker safety, and environmental laws. So too with good government measures. The Freedom of Information Act, and key provisions of the Ethics in Government Act, apply only to the executive branch, not Congress. Even when lawmakers agree, under pressure, to cover themselves, they strip the laws of all meaning by arranging for cozy enforcement by their own staff.

The attitude of being above the law corrupts the legislative process at its heart. Incumbents claim that Congress must be exempt from the law so as not to fall under the control of the executive or judicial branches. This makes no more sense than arguing that Congress should not be allowed to pass legislation affecting judges or cabinet members, lest those officials become subservient to the legislature. Separation of powers means that Congress makes the laws, not that it is exempt from them. Indeed, that doctrine dictates that Congress keep its hands off the administration and adjudication of laws. More narrowly, Congressmen cite the constitutional protection against being questioned elsewhere for speech or debate in Congress, but speeches are rarely the issue.

In most cases there is no constitutional issue in applying the law to Congress. True, we don't want an FBI or IRS conspiracy to coerce legislators with threats of investigation, but it is difficult to see what constitutional damage would be wrought by, for instance, OSHA inspectors visiting congressional offices. Republican Rep. John Boehner of Ohio invited just such an inspection of his office on a voluntary basis in the summer of 1992, uncovering numerous violations of worker safety standards. In fact, most of the OSHA "violations" were clearly insignificant, proving Rep. Boehner's point that making Congress subject to the laws it approves would provoke more attention to the problems a well-intentioned law may present. More importantly, making Congress live under the laws it passes would drive home a point that too many legislators have forgotten: they are not rulers but servants. If Congress believes an investigation is politically motivated or otherwise improper, it has plenty of tools to fight back. Legislators and their employees are required to present any subpoenas delivered to them to the full House or Senate. If some constitutional principle is at stake, Congress can object and interpose its institutional prerogatives at that point rather than declaring before the fact that Congressmen are above the law. The minority of Hill workers who have legislative responsibilities may be a special case, for which there is a ready model: the treatment of political appointees in the executive branch. Those appointees are covered by all the laws applying to other employees, but they can nonetheless be fired, with no practical appeal, for policy reasons or violations of confidence.

Congress should adopt a blanket congressional coverage statute, and House and Senate rules should require all legislation to cover Congress unless there is a specific, recorded vote to the contrary. If Congress insists on maintaining its own enforcement offices (as some executive branch agencies are allowed to do), then it should use enforcement standards identical to those used in other government agencies, to provide an objective standard for measuring congressional compliance. Court appeals must be allowed, and most especially, Congressmen should not be permitted to escape jury trials. With a jury, Congress is not subject to another branch of government, but to citizens. Businesses fear unpredictable verdicts in lawsuits as much as the specific requirements of regulatory legislation. It would be productive for Congress, no less than the rest of us, to contemplate the same possibility when crafting vague laws.

Apply Freedom of Information. If there is a single law that most needs be applied to Congress it is the Freedom of Information Act. Congress gets away with many abuses simply because no one can find out about them: the cozy relationships that comprise the Barnumocracy, the petty acts of retribution that keep bureaucrats in thrall of Capitol Hill. If Congressmen and their staffs were required to keep adequate records and to make them available to the public, many congressional abuses would go away overnight, and questionable behavior would be subject to the informed judgment of voters. Again, the light of accountability is the key to reform.

End the Constituent Service Racket. Casework, helping constituents solve problems with the government, is Congress's number-one occupation. Stopping it will do wonders to restore a legislative focus to Congress. If constituents are continually being shafted, Congress should fix the systemic problems rather than patching up faulty operations one problem at a time. As it is, Congress turns legislative power over to bureaucrats, then stands ready to apply bandages when the regulations hurt. We're supposed to express gratitude by voting for them. This process removes any incentive for Congress to limit the size of government or to fix the problems that cause voters so many headaches. In fact, bad government gets Congressmen reelected. Large reductions in staff, especially in personal staffs, are probably the only way to achieve this goal.

For those inevitable cases where paperwork is lost, or constituents confused, an ombudsman system, either within agencies or as an arm of Congress, would be far preferable to the current arrangement. Short of stopping, Congress could come clean about casework. All manner of scandalous political favors are covered by the little-old-lady-with-the-lost-check ploy. Congressmen should be required to report all correspondence with, and phone calls to, executive agencies periodically in the Congressional Record. If it is all just honest casework, Congressmen should be proud. If they're not, we can only assume they have something to hide. If Congress won't take this step itself, then the President should order executive agencies to log and report congressional contacts as public matters.

Establish Fair and Open Procedures. One reason Congress has difficulty acting on important issues is that its committees, dominated by special interests, are allowed to bottle up popular legislation. When bills do reach the House floor, controversial amendments are often blocked. As we saw in Chapter One, through a variety of ruses, Members are able to stake out positions on both sides of an issue, voting one way while doing the opposite, or even not voting at all on controversial issues. In this process, too, accountability is lost. House and Senate rules should be revised to produce a more orderly, fair, and open process. This can start with setting the legislative agenda.

Frustration over important legislation getting bogged down has led some to recommend giving new scheduling powers to a few House and Senate leaders. This would only open the door to new abuses. A better system would give every lawmaker a voice, and stake, in setting an agenda. This could be accomplished with a brief debate on legislation when it is introduced, a system followed in early Congresses. Simple bills were approved, silly ones disposed of, and complex ones sent to a committee. (The Senate retains vestiges of this procedure: If a Senator objects to referral of a bill to committee it is placed on the calendar immediately.)

Reviving this procedure would allow Congress to decide on an agenda openly and enforce it. In referring a bill, Members could instruct committees to complete action within a given time or indicate in a general way how a bill should be amended. The clutter of congressional calendars would be reduced, and frivolous proposals cut down, as sponsors would be loath to endure their colleagues' taunts for introducing pointless legislation. The complexity of bills would probably be reduced since simpler measures would be more likely to be approved. If debating every bill seems like too much, Congress might allow the procedure to be invoked selectively by the leadership of either party or by a significant number of Members.

The House Rules Committee, which sets ground rules for debating bills on the House floor, too frequently bends procedures in favor of the Democrat majority, especially by blocking politically contentious amendments. While some variation in rules may be necessary, a few standard procedures should be developed to cover most bills. Changes in those standard rules should require a super-majority (60 percent or more) vote. Absent an agenda reform such as the one described above, significant minorities within the House should be given a greater voice in what legislation is considered. Currently, action can be forced on legislation if a majority of the House (normally 218 Members) signs a "discharge petition." Because the petition is kept secret, however, voters have a hard time keeping score: Representatives can claim to support legislation while refusing to do what is necessary to get it enacted. Discharge petitions should be made public, and the threshold for forcing action should be lowered. There is no reason why the House should not consider legislation supported by, say, a third of its Members.

Senate rules, which already give more protections to minorities, need fewer revisions. In fact, changes to make Senate procedure more centrally controlled, as in the House, should be avoided.

Finally, congressional rules should be revised to make votes more meaningful. The House practice of approving legislation or amendments without votes ("deeming") should be prohibited. Conference committees, which are supposed to work out differences between House and Senate versions of bills, should not be allowed to practice stealth legislation by deleting provisions both bodies have agreed to or adding new material neither had approved.

Cut Committees. Much mischief in pork and micromanagement is conducted by committees independent of the knowledge or will of the majority of

Members. Several previous reforms have limited committee and subcommittee numbers, but like weeds, they require periodic clearing. The rearrangement of committee jurisdiction is relatively unimportant as long as the numbers are significantly reduced, by half or more. The resulting broader jurisdictions would promote a more integrated approach to lawmaking. Congressmen would sit on a handful of panels, rather than as many as 23, as is the case with one Senator today. Among other salutary effects, this would increase the attention Congressmen give to each committee position, and therefore reduce the role staff plays.

Members who are concerned about the concentration of power in the hands of fewer chairmen should impose term limits on those chairmen as suggested by Oklahoma Democratic Rep. Dave McCurdy. While McCurdy's proposal is in the form of a change in House rules, it is the Republican and Democratic caucuses in each body that designate chairmen and ranking members. There is no reason why those party organizations should not move on their own to limit the tenure of committee chairmen, or even of all committee members. Over the course of six years or so even the most ambitious chairman should be able to advance a legislative agenda. Allowing Members to remain chairmen, or senior committee members, for long periods simply allows the natural process of forging common links with bureaucrats and interest groups to thwart the detachment necessary to the legislative role.

Limit terms, sessions, staff, committees, chairmen, spending and pork; apply all laws to Congress, open up congressional procedure and junk the casework scam.

This is an ambitious program, but one that will work, one that can be achieved through continuing public pressure. The point of these reforms is not to attack Congress but to rejuvenate it, and, by restoring accountability, to rejuvenate American government with it. The reforms point in one direction: bringing Congress back to its assigned task, legislation. Only by stopping many current activities can this succeed. Congressmen will argue that the activities we want them to cease are necessary to control the huge federal bureaucracy, and in this they are probably right. Surely, however, it is not a matter of asking Congress to give up control and leave bureaucrats roaming at will but to give Members incentives to limit the powers they delegate to that bureaucracy. Thus doing, they will at once reclaim their legislative responsibilities and political dignity.

Make Congress legislate. That is its job. A Congress that makes law through fair and open legislative procedure is a Congress that can be held accountable for its actions. A Congress accountable to the voters is a Congress that, by definition, will do the right thing. A Congress that legislates will be a Congress no longer in need of reform.

INDEX

HERITAGE PUBLICATIONS

☐ Please send me a FREE catalog of The Heritage
Foundation publications.

☐ One-year subscription to *Policy Review*, Heritage's news-
making quarterly magazine ($22.00).

☐ "Should Congress be Above the Law?" *Backgrounder
#965*, by Dan Greenberg ($3.50).

☐ "Why America Needs a Balanced Budget Amendment"
Backgrounder Update #204,
by Daniel J. Mitchell ($2.00).

☐ "How Your New Taxes will Fund New Pork"
Backgrounder #954, by Scott A. Hodge ($3.50).

☐ "Slowing the Spending Stampede: A Five-Day Waiting
Period for Congress" *Backgrounder #951*, by Dan
Greenberg ($3.50).

☐ "A Guide to H.R. 2434: The Putting Jobs and
The American Family First Act of 1993" *Issue Bulletin
#179*, by Scott A. Hodge ($3.50).

☐ "A Guide to the Clinton Health Plan" *Heritage Talking
Points*, by Robert E. Moffit ($3.50).

THE HERITAGE FOUNDATION
214 Massachusetts Ave., NE
Washington, DC 20002

Please send me the Heritage publications checked above.
Enclosed is my check for $_____ or please charge
my ☐ Mastercard ☐ Visa

No._____Exp. Date _____

Signature _____

Name _____

Address _____

City _____ St. _____ Zip _____

PLEASE JOIN THE HERITAGE FOUNDATION

For only $15 you can become a member of the most influential conservative think tank in America. You'll receive a quarterly newsletter, a handsome membership card, and surveys that tell Congress what you think on important issues facing America. Your contribution will help Heritage's fight to restore Congress to the role our Nation's Founding Fathers intended.

. . . or Join Heritage's CongressWatchers

For your $100 contribution you become a member of the Heritage CongressWatchers. *You'll receive a free copy of each publication we issue about Congress, and updates on Heritage's U.S. Congress Assessment Project which will expand our common-sense ideas for reform,* in addition to all the benefits of Heritage membership.

THE HERITAGE FOUNDATION, Attention: Carsten Walter
214 Massachusetts Ave., NE
Washington, DC 20002

☐ Yes. I want to become a member of The Heritage Foundation and help in the fight to restore Congress to the role our Founding Fathers intended.

I've chosen the following membership option:

☐ $15 membership fee

☐ $100 to join the Heritage CongressWatchers Club (please also send me your latest Heritage paper on Congress).

Enclosed is my check for $_____

Name _____

Address _____

City _____ St. _____ Zip _____